"Dr. Janice Presser provides refreshing, direct ⸺
that leaders and teams face in today's world ⸺
real life experience applies an essential cran⸺
creating and leading enabled teams."

Harry Tucker ~ Fortune 25 Strategy A⸺

"Dr. Janice is a constant source of inspiration and education; I learn something new with each candor-filled post and tweet. I'm not the only one who considers Dr. Janice a premier mentor and colleague. Her presence in the #InternPro community is widely felt; our young careerists love her direct style, sincerity and passion for helping others create a fulfilling career and life."

Mark Babbitt, CEO ~ YouTern.com

"I've taken the Teamability exercise. It is both a unique testing concept and a measurement model for identifying an individual's set of personal strengths and challenges. Teamability is like seeing yourself, and your creativity, leadership and communication skills, in an 'insight mirror of truth.' When Dr. Janice's customized analysis of your operating style, motivational drivers, and abilities to connect with others is layered onto the predictive metrics, the result is creation of an honest, straightforward, and highly actionable behavioral portrait."

Michael W. Lowenstein ~ Ph.D., CMC, Chief Research Officer
The Relational Capital Group

"I'm impressed with Dr. Janice's thought-provoking work. Her commitment to the future of work and leaders of all shapes and sizes is nothing short of inspiring. What is the future of teamwork? I'm relying on her careful research, incredible insight and humor to guide the way."

Meghan M. Biro ~ CEO and Founder
TalentCulture Consulting Group

"I spent most of my career working with people and organizations that were seeking better ways to hire, organize, and optimize teams. The methods were well-intentioned, but too often of low-impact with occasional flashes of brilliance. This was all before Dr. Janice Presser unleashed her 'technology of teaming', which gives a hiring team leader qualitative descriptions that paint a clear picture of how a person will fit into a team. I've experienced Teamability myself, and I know many CEOs who require its use BEFORE they bring candidates in for interviews."

Larry Evans ~ Co-Founder
Right Management Consultants

"*Dr. Janice has been a refreshing voice of economically sound reason when it comes to teamwork and the world of work. Her engaging humor and inclusive insight is something the TalentCulture #TChat Community longs to hear each week, and now we'll have it in perpetuity with her new book.*"

Kevin W. Grossman ~ #TChat Co-founder
HR Writer and Peoplefluent Director

"*Since I've known Janice Presser, she's unfailingly given me powerful and practical mentoring and guidance. Her wellspring of wisdom is vast – and more importantly – it's relevant to our world. Dr. Presser is one of those rare visionaries and outliers who offers something truly compelling and worthy of understanding: objective, constructive truth.*"

Bill Puryear ~ Developer of Leadership, Teams & Organizations

"*Team-building…yes, Dr. Janice wrote the book on the topic. I highly recommend her introduction of Teamability to your staff or volunteer teams, and you will not be disappointed in the results. It leaves you hungry for more information as you begin to transform your project teams to optimize results.*"

Randi Mayes ~ Executive Director
International Legal Technology Association

"*She may be petite in stature but Dr. Presser is a giant in shaping the future of the workplace. Dr. J has impacted my clients profoundly, and Teamability – her technology of teaming – is providing a competitive advantage and real business value.*"

Tom Thomson ~ President
Sanford Rose Associates – Franklin

"*Dr. J is so intelligently perceptive that she can identify your Role in life within minutes of meeting you. Her technology of Teamability is even more amazing, and has much to offer to professionals, teams, and entire organizations.*"

Dennis D'Andrea ~ President
D3 Financial Group

"*I'm at an age where I do not seek or typically need mentors, but I make one exception: Janice Presser. Her work in identifying how people work together is amazingly insightful. It reminds me of her…smart, visionary, and effective.*"

Greg Sparzo ~ Managing Director
Horton International

"Thanks to @DrJanice and Teamability, the art of the possible in team building and development is changed from glossy fiction to a practical, non-fiction handbook."

Ray Celli ~ President
Optiera, Inc.

"Teamability is one of the most disruptive innovations I have seen in years. This technology has the potential to minimize friction in a company, and enables teams to solve problems and build internal resilience. Through the technology and working with Dr. Janice, I have learned to identify the Roles of people that will make the right contributions, at the right time, in the right way. If you are a leader, you simply must see what this technology can do to propel you forward, faster."

Natalie Sweeney ~ Business Innovation Strategy Consultant
Highmark

"In a field where the academic and the practical rarely meet, Dr. Janice has used extensive research to develop a set of human relations metrics and methods that are easy to use and apply, and bring sustainable and reproducible results in the real world."

Fred Wilf ~ Technology Lawyer

"Professionals who wouldn't buy a laptop without thorough analysis will routinely hire key colleagues on quasi-intuition. DrJanice and Teamability can end all that!"

Lowell Hussey ~ Odemax.com

"Dr. J has broken through the organizational fixation on optimizing functional excellence to the detriment of nurturing and accelerating team goals and performance. Teamability stresses the work group dynamics that are critical to achieving process improvement and the key tenets of Six Sigma. Finally, real focus."

John A. Vigna ~ CEO and President
SISD, LLC

"Rarely is an individual's vision so closely matched with what they ultimately deliver. Dr. Presser has consistently surpassed the mark. Her discoveries around teams and workforce dynamics are truly game-changing."

Darryl King ~ Minister of Education and Leadership Council Member
Lake Norman Baptist Church, Huntersville NC

"Janice Presser, or Dr. J as she's known here, is one of Philadelphia's great entrepreneurs: persistent, nimble, quick to read the market and pivot rapidly, multi-talented, a master of building the village every entrepreneur needs, smart as a whip, fun and witty. Her blogs and other communications are must-reads for entrepreneurs at all stages of development because her content consistently provides something insightful, relevant and usable. Caution: Try her posts just once, and you're hooked."

Jaine Lucas ~ Executive Director, Innovation and Entrepreneurship Institute Temple University – Fox School of Business

"Dr. J, her team, and approach to employee selection, employee placement and team development is a valuable asset to our company as we focus on culture change to facilitate our growth and sustainability in the future. The easily understood, easily translatable, and easily applied 'where the rubber meets the road' tools, insight and support are valuable components of our quest."

Ernie Inmon ~ Chairman and CEO U. S. Axle, Inc.

"Janice Presser and her team have brought a completely new and refreshed way to look at talent. I have used Teamability reports before in my consulting practice and regularly since I joined Sabadell in 2011…we don't hire anyone until we learn about them with this great technology."

Edmundo Hoffens ~ Executive VP and Chief Human Resources Officer Sabadell Americas

"Janice is an exceptional innovator whose work, and its unique processes, guides the creation of successful management teams."

Richard Miller ~ VP Marketing and Communications Iowa Innovation Corporation

"@DrJanice has followers far and wide, but those who have met her in person realize that there's a lot more to like about Dr. Janice Presser than just her wit. At some point in the not-too-distant future, the world will be knocking on her door, wanting to learn all there is to know about teaming, and Teamability!"

Marc Kramer ~ Founder and President Commercial Deposit Insurance Agency, www.cdiaus.com

"Dr. Janice generates contagious positive energy and spirit! She is incredibly passionate about her work and has done an outstanding job of educating our organization on the benefits of utilizing Teamability reports. This technology has become a part of who we are as a company, and has been instrumental in our recruitment decisions."

Lauren Boegner ~ Vice President of Human Resources
Preferred Sands

"Janice has a knack for exposing what really matters in any situation or topic she addresses. She has educated me and some of my clients on the vagaries of human interaction, with positive results well beyond any normal expectations."

Don Patrick ~ President
SRA Executive Search – Norcross

"The brilliant work Dr. Janice has produced is having a profound effect on business efficiency and productivity. Its application in the social sphere is improving relationship clarity and mutual respect. Identifying people best able to remain calm in trying circumstances results in harmony and positive team synergy. Her vision of economic benefits and a better world for all is in the making, through the technology of teaming."

Tom Talaba ~ President, Ontario, Inc.
Toronto, Ontario, Canada

"I'm flattered that sections of @DrJanice first appeared in my publication, InnovationDaily. But that doesn't change the fact that Janice is a keen observer of human interaction, or that the technology she co-created has the potential to change the way we see ourselves in the workplace and how teams are managed, all for the better."

Richard A. Bendis ~ Founder and CEO
InnovationAmerica

"Thanks to Dr. Presser and her breakthrough technology, I can easily access information and methods that raise organizational performance to a high level. She also helped me understand how I can be the most effective leader for my team. Take my word for it, her wisdom will improve your bottom line!"

RD Whitney ~ Executive Director, Institute of Finance and Management
Diversified Business Communications

@DrJanice

Thoughts & Tweets On Leadership, Teamwork & Teamability®

Dr. Janice Presser

TEN TREES PRESS
Philadelphia

ISBN 978-0578124513

Originally published in paperback by Ten Trees Press, May 2013
P. O. Box 1396, Doylestown, PA 18901

Edited by: Mark Talaba
Art Direction & Design: Jerad MacLean (CanyonGraphicArts.com)
Production: Jay McPhillips (www.JayMcPhillips.com)
Photography: Tom Thomson
Illustrations: David Kelly

Printed in the United States of America

To the team.

It's all about the team.

@DrJanice

Contents

@DrJanice: The real key to success is knowing who you are... and who you are not. #wisdom

Introduction

I was neither born nor raised to be a leader. Not a CEO. Not the founder of a startup company. Not the architect of a new technology.

I was expected to be like my mother and the other women who started their families in 1946, the first full year of peace. I was meant to be a lady with a wardrobe of gloves and hats and aprons. My ride was to be a baby carriage. And my career aspirations, if any, were to be a teacher because then I could have summers off with my children. But the path was not to endure: as the fifties turned into the sixties neither the peace nor the place of women would remain the same. Hardly anything, for that matter, would ever be the same.

Unfortunately, in corporate America, reality was slower to catch up. When applying for my first jobs I, unlike my pants-wearing counterparts, was given a typing test. (This was before the invention of the pantsuit.)

Time went on, as did my life. Suffice it to say, many things happened: some were planned, some were unexpected, some were miracles. They are reflected in what I've written here.

The following chapters are arranged in three sections, roughly organized around the concepts of leading, teaming, and a new technology of which I was the co-creator during the past quarter-century, called Teamability®. Throughout, these thoughts are punctuated by some of the many tweets I've tweeted as @DrJanice. They became favorites of mine because of someone (or some ones) kind enough to let me know this or that thought had arrived just when they needed to hear it.

With my best wishes for your success, as you define it.

Dr. Janice Presser
April 19, 2013

PS: I took the liberty of adding an unusually long afterword. I hope it may help you to discover your personal next level through whatever great challenges you face.

@DrJanice: Everyone communicates. Not everyone listens. #justsaying

Part 1: Thoughts & Tweets

I started blogging in 2007 and tweeting in 2008. Having done five books for major publishers and written a slew of articles over the years, not to mention a dissertation, it wasn't hard to come up with words. The challenge was to condense things that had been taking up an inordinate amount of headspace.

Here are some of my thoughts. If we ever meet, we could easily spend a week talking about any of them. And I think I would be listening more than speaking.

@DrJanice: You don't need anyone's permission to lead. #leadership

There are 10 commandments for becoming a leader. I didn't get them off of tablets. But they will get you to your promised land.

Ten Commandments for Becoming a Leader

1. Assume that people have the best interests of the organization in their intentions.

2. Be forgiving, even when people make mistakes.

3. Be merciful when people make big mistakes.

4. Be compassionate: don't place people in tempting circumstances.

5. Be gracious, even to those who don't return it.

6. Be slow to anger when people disobey.

7. Be abundantly kind and assume people mean well.

8. Never renege on your word.

9. Remember the times when people do something right.

10. Always allow people to repent their error, carelessness or apathy and forgive them.

By the way, even if you decide you'd rather not be a leader, follow these anyway. You'll have a more satisfying, less stressful life.

@DrJanice: Is part of the problem with communication that we have con-versations when we should have pro-versations? #justasking

I've always loved Peanuts cartoons. You can share them with anyone and while they are often profound, they're never offensive. Naturally, I resonate with Lucy, outspoken and bossy as she is. Except in the matter of Light.

Leading into the Light

There is a famous old Peanuts cartoon. Linus, the budding philosopher, quotes "It is better to light one candle rather than curse the darkness", whereupon Lucy, ever the pessimist, yells something like, "You stupid darkness!"

Before you choose your favorite (and yes, one choice is more socially desirable) consider the advantages of being a Lucy.

- You never have to expend much energy finding the candle and lighting it.

- You don't have to actually achieve anything, so you don't have to put forth any effort.

- You won't have to challenge any of your old beliefs, even the ones that make you miserable.

Are you with me? There is a choice here to be made. To do something positive that causes the light to be lit – or to curse it for not lighting itself.

Make no mistake about it: there is a lot of darkness in the world. You may not be feeling very positive about searching for light, especially if this has been a particularly dark time for you. If it has, the only positive thing may be that you are tired of cursing it.

So here are my three best suggestions for making sure that even in the darkness, you leave room for some light.

- One candle might not seem like much in a sea of darkness, so find other holders of light. They are all around, but even if you can't see them, their flames will keep yours lit.

- If you find yourself surrounded by cursers, refuse to join. Instead, consider turning their curses into kisses by thanking them for their caring about whatever it is that they are cursing.

- Remember, curses pass the tongue quickly but linger in the atmosphere. Before you are tempted to curse the darkness, look around. Do you really want to snuff out other people's candles, or would you rather let yourself be warmed by their light?

Just one more reminder: the direction a leader takes is the direction in which their team will follow them.

**@DrJanice: Be good at what you are good at.
Nothing else makes sense. #career**

*I stopped writing resumes when I realized I was much happier
starting a business. For one, you don't have to interview when
you're the boss. And since if you're successful you don't have to keep
your resume updated, it's all the more joyful. But that's just not true
for everyone.*

How to Keep Your Resume Out of the Circular File

I looked at a senior executive's resume — something I never
do, but he is such a nice guy and his Teamability report was so
good, I figured I'd do it, just for research. He's a consultant now,
but he's been in senior management the latter part of his career.
With the economy improving, he's on the prowl and some
lucky company is going to get him. After he fixes his resume…

So I'm going to offer my advice here, in hopes that if you are
looking for a new C level job (or any job for that matter) that it
will help you too.

First, put your address on it so it doesn't look like you are living
in your car. I know you have a lot of experience and you want
to cram it into two pages because somewhere there is a two
page rule, but really, this is not the place to skimp.

Then think about a better title or tag line. No one will read
everything you wrote because resumes are inherently boring,
especially compared to some of the funnier jokes your friends
sent you today or you read on your intern's monitor.

Put your industry right up there in the title. I know you want to
appear flexible but executive recruiters care about industry. A lot.
That's how they make money, specializing in an industry. So get
it on there.

Also use the title you expect or want. Like Lord High Executioner or Ruler of the Queen's Navee.

So your title will be something like Chief Financial Officer, Aerospace Industry, or Senior Organizational Development Leader, 18 years in Banking. Don't use a number if you think it isn't a good one. (I don't know what a good number is. This is something you need to be comfortable with.)

Rework your opening summary paragraph so it doesn't sound like Dogbert wrote it. (I like Dogbert but you have to make this very concrete because it isn't going to be read by people like us.) Short sentences. Really. People don't read. Okay, make that most people. And they are screening your resume. Make. Them. Happy.

Then make the bullet points pop. Make each one count and make them very different. No Dogbert. No hackneyed words. If you don't know which words not to use, read Dilbert (www. Dilbert.com).

Be more specific on Core Competencies, if you have a section with them. Make it reflect you and no one else. If we were talking marketing we would be talking differentiation.

Now you're ready to prune your list of past employment. Be brutal. Only keep what will keep the reader reading. That's a summary statement, what you did, how it made the company happy. That's it. And leave off your first jobs if they don't contribute anything. Same with non-degree training and such.

Now you have room to GIVE ME MARGINS!!! People who actually might want to talk to you will appreciate a place to make notes. Or to doodle. Whatever, it will look better.

And remember, especially if you are a senior executive, that the hiring manager reading your resume is likely to have significant experience. That's HR-speak for 'old enough to need reading glasses'. So pump up that font size. Please.

And good luck!

@DrJanice: Be yourself. Period. #KISS

I belong to a senior executive group where there are always some people looking for a new opportunity. Maybe it's just that people like to complain to me, but no one ever had a nice word to say about an interview. So I answered their unspoken question.

Why Interviews Suck

Notice that I am making a statement, not asking a question. There is no question about it. Interviews suck. And it doesn't matter if you are the interviewer, the interviewee, or someone else who's been sucked into the process.

There are three simple reasons.

First, interviews are very much like blind dates. Both sides get a lot of hype upfront, and most of it is inaccurate or misleading. Think back to the last time you bought into: "…and he's so good to his mother" or "…but she has a wonderful personality." Is that any different from "…he's an undervalued property" or "…you'll really grow with this company"?

The bottom line is that interviews are a form of assessment, and no matter how structured or fair you think you are being, they are neither standardized nor objective. Even if you are using behavioral interviewing techniques, the information you retain about each candidate will still have been filtered through your personal frame of reference and unconscious biases. And just like the date who seemed like a perfect fit – until their quirks, or their temper, or some other undocumented features began to show up – there are people who have become experts at getting hired by NOT being themselves during the interview process. (Did you know there are dating coaches and interview coaches that drill people in how to get lucky?)

Second, for various reasons, the scales tend to tilt in favor of people who are least likely to be great team players. Poorly defined job scope? Insufficient resources? Unrealistic performance expectations? A great team player will raise relevant issues for discussion. A bad team player will tell you just what you want to hear. To make matters worse, all parties to the interview process have the same desired outcome, which no one will openly admit: *they just want to get it over with!*

- For HR or a staff recruiter, the harder the hiring manager is to deal with, the stronger this desire becomes.

- For an external recruiter, the desire to close and move on is variable: retained search, "No problem"; contingency, "Excellent choice! When will my check be mailed?"

- The interviewer(s) will push for rapid progress to the 'right' decision, despite the fact that the same process has proven faulty in the past.

- And lastly, the candidates (depending on their employment status, how shaky they think their present situation is, and any number of other factors) want a job, a great job, the perfect job, or at least one that they can survive until they land somewhere else. All this pressure favors candidates who are easy to fall in love with, instead of the people who are the most capable of adding value to the team.

Third, the very best person for the job rarely gets picked. Why? Let's go back to dating for a moment. Did you know that the surest way to hook up with the wrong person is to look for someone who matches your personal want list? (This is a fact based on research, not folklore.) Think about it: can a list of experiences, skills, and physical attributes predict the quality of interpersonal behavior? Certainly not! In order to get a positive I.D. on a good team player, you need to know something about how the person will behave when working with others to overcome obstacles and achieve common goals. Unfortunately, that's not what we get from interviewing.

Then there are the interminable screenings to match candidates to a job req, i.e., the 'want list'. And since screening is rarely done by the person who is doing the hiring, potential candidates with slightly different, yet truly unique and excellent qualifications often get kicked to the curb. The longer and more complex the interview process and the more people involved, the more likely the process will produce a lowest common denominator selection. Example: we know of a senior level executive who worked for well over a year to convince a competitor's top salesman to jump ship, only to lose this guaranteed star player in an off target and humiliating (for the candidate) interdepartmental stress interview. Bottom line: interview survivors may be the ones who best tolerate non-productivity, who thrive on petty corporate politics, and/or who blow the biggest smokescreen.

As the saying goes, "If you keep on doing what you've always done, you'll keep on getting what you've always got." If you want productive teams, you need to be able to identify the best team players. Do that BEFORE you make big investments in a questionable interview process and risk a long term commitment to the wrong person.

Some aspects of interviewing may always suck, but the outcomes will be a lot better if you limit it to the candidates who really know how to team!

**@DrJanice: Key words, key words, key words –
what would you use if you were searching for you?
#justasking**

*Someone joked that I probably don't like fiction either, but that's
not true. My secret vice is reading mysteries on my iPad. If that ever
becomes a crime, there is a record somewhere of everything I've ever
downloaded. Even the ones that weren't that great were better than
reading a resume.*

Why I Don't Read Resumes

I got a resume a couple of weeks ago from an out of work
executive. I'm going to share the five sentences in the summary
statement and maybe together we can figure out what it tells us
– and what it means. Let's try the first one:

- *Human Resources Professional with strong business acumen
  focused on enabling business success through people, experienced
  in both small start-up as well as multinational Fortune 200.*

What do you think?

(Sure, strong business acumen could be there – or not. How do
you measure that and, more important, how do you know this
is actually the person responsible for the referenced business
success? Most business accomplishments consist of interactions
between an individual, other individuals and the outside world –
also known as the vagaries of the market.)

- *Multinational experience including a three and one half year
  assignment living in Asia Pacific as well as extensive business
  travel in Europe.*

What's your take on this?

(Maybe someone in the home office disliked this person and
sent them as far away as possible? It happens!)

- *Change agent and Business Partner building and aligning Human Resources with the business to affect positive business results.*

Your thoughts?

(Change Agent sounds so sixties. I'm not so sure about being a partner, and trying to change people, AND aligning human resources. Sounds like this one wants to be a partner in the sense of making all the decisions.)

- *Expanding high potential promotable pools of talent for current and future business needs.*

What do you think?

(When I first read this I got an image of the person pumping people full of air and floating them in a giant pool. With a crystal ball.)

- *Driving enhancements in employee/leadership engagement resulting in higher retention of top talent and lower undesirable turnover.*

For me, not so much. You?

(Again with the driving! I think he or she thinks this will make me think of him or her as a strong leader. But what if the culture of the organization favors cordial citizens over pile-drivers?)

Here's what it comes down to, for me. Two things.

First, what's truly important to hiring is impossible to express in a resume or to figure out from the process I've been thinking of as 'resume divination'. None of us can tell much about anyone from a resume. For instance, you shouldn't assume the person who sent it even wrote it, and research has shown that well over half of all resumes contain material of questionable origin. Then there are typos, which indicate that either the person didn't read it well enough to catch them all, or that the written word is not a strength. In either instance, do you care? People who are great at fixing the little details aren't necessarily going to focus on the big picture, so first decide what you really need and then figure out if you're asking for the impossible. Do you really want someone who plans brilliantly for the far off future AND picks up on the smallest bits of administrivia? Or how about a super salesperson who's extremely organized? You might get someone who is great at neither.

Second, if you have to write a resume and you have trouble creating perky phrases, don't worry. You can buy even better lines in career books at your local bookstore, or get them at the library.

Happy wordsmithing!

@DrJanice: Learn what's coming and if it's a train, switch rails!

People think that because I was a family therapist at one point in my life, and at another I wrote five books on family relations, that I know what I'm talking about. Count my daughter out of that group.

Even Experts Sing the Blues

It's all about fit. What you need to know is, will this person fit? Will they do what's needed in a pinch – will they come through for you – but mostly, will they do the job you're hiring them for really, really well. I can tell you one thing. If you are expecting them to do something most of the time, most days, make sure it's something they love, something they truly have passion about. People do best what they like best and people like best what they do best. That's it. If they don't like it, they won't do it well. So how do you know? Resumes won't tell you and neither will an interview.

Nor, if you're like me, will even living with the candidate give you much of an edge. Here is my true story.

Actually, this is my true confession. I am a terrible mother, former HR person, and former family therapist.

The company where my daughter was working had been bought by American Express, and they moved her division to a beautiful location in Arizona. She was offered a relocation package and it was very exciting. Then she told me she wasn't going. "I'm not leaving my friends and I'm not leaving my family," she told me. I thought she was crazy to pass on such a great opportunity, but I kept my mouth closed and just offered her some help. She hadn't finished college so I was prepared to support her through.

17

I asked her what she wanted to do. She said, "I just want to help people." I said "That's great, become a behavioral scientist. We help people." She said, "No you don't." I said "Okay, become a social worker. They help people." She said, very slowly so I would get it, "You don't understand. I just want to *help* people."

Ok, I gave up. I told her to call Dr. Jack and ask him to give her what we were then working on, the project that eventually produced Teamability. And I told her to get back to me when she decided what she was doing with her life. She really was driving me crazy since she was still living in the room that was supposed to be my home office.

So she did it and Jack called me, laughing his head off. "No wonder you don't understand her – you don't even particularly like people like her," he said. I swear I could hear him cackling. His nickname is Wizard. I was crestfallen. "This is my baby," I whined to him. "I gave birth to her at home, I nursed her forever, I took care of her, I LOVE her," I went on and on. He said "Yes, but you don't like her."

So I said, "Okay, what is she?" "Communicator," he said. I argued with him. I couldn't believe it – my child? Not a Vision Former? I asked what she was talking about. What does she want to do? Customer service was his answer. I was appalled and told him. "It's a horrible job." He said, "Yes, for you." He took me to task like only a good friend can do reminding me that I wrote about this stuff and helped OTHER people and he generally kept beating me down till I cried Uncle.

Eventually I gave in and started to treat her with the kind of respect a Communicator wants. And today she is the Queen of Customer Service for the luckiest company on earth. And she is a much better employee...errrr, daughter. Since then, I've helped thousands of other people understand their employees better. Some have even been parents. I know what I'm talking about when it comes to other people's kids.

The moral of this story is that no matter how many years of training you've had and how good you think you should be, you aren't. The best assessments are indirect and you can't do that in an interview, even a behavioral interview, much less the reading or even divination of a resume. And everything you do in an interview or reading goes through all the filters of your mind's experience.

My dear daughter is very smart but only had one year of college. She just didn't like it. She is up front that she is not ambitious. But her customers feel so comfortable with her, they open up about other problems they are having with the products they need. She wants to help them so she takes every opportunity to learn more about the products. Because her customers trust that she is truly concerned about them, they let her know of other needs and she finds the products that will help them. She doesn't think of this as upselling and when I pointed out to her that that was exactly what she was doing she got a little miffed with me and explained that she was just helping them and had no interest in sales.

She's not just for helping customers either – she has other talents. When she realized that there wasn't enough information to really help customers, she started writing little cheat sheets on the things she learned and started sharing them with her co-workers. I still don't understand her very well because she's so different from me. But finally I can appreciate her, respect her, and support her choices.

I guess I owe you another true confession here. If I hadn't listened to her Teamability report but had, instead, insisted on being an idiot mom/idiot HR person/idiot behavioral scientist relying on my clever resume divination and interview skills, this story would not have had such a happy ending.

@DrJanice: 99% of #innovation is not saying no.

Seems to me that innovation is the natural state of people or we never would have advanced through the ages from stone to bronze to iron to wherever we're going now. This was inspired by a friend who works for Inno Vader.

Who Put the 'No' in Your Innovation?

You dreamt up something completely new. It is so cool that people don't even know they need it yet. But, like their iPad, once they try it, they'll forget they ever had a life without it.

It was a fit for your line of business, so – with great hopes swelling in your chest – you brought it to your teammate, your manager, or even the Vice President of Innovation, and it got shot down before you even had a chance to explain the vision, or the strategy, or the compelling need it would serve.

You're a grownup, and you can take rejection. But still, it grinds you. It's one thing when people give an idea a fair shake, and maybe it doesn't fly because one or the other decision-makers isn't in the know, but this time it was clear that they were simply in the NO!

What's an innovator to do?

First identify the naysayer. Was it one of these usual suspects?

- Nano Teamer: This is the person who is so into teamwork that they spend more time talking about it than doing it. A favorite expression: "There's no 'I' in team." A frequent tendency: hanging around where things are happening and taking credit for results that were actually produced by other people. Motivation: If it will make someone else look good, kill it.

- Mini Manager: There are managers who are team players, and there are managers who play their team. The latter type prefers to be the source of all great ideas and all good will. Anyone else who dares to tread on that turf is regarded with suspicion, or worse, and will be dealt with severely.

- Inno Vader: Like Inno's big brother Darth, he (or she) believes that the purpose of decision making power is to punch the other person's lights out. It's ironic that some of the people who have Innovation in their job title seem to be preoccupied with controlling innovation rather than facilitating it. It's a little like the VC or Angel investor who thinks, "I have the money. Therefore, I get to decide because that makes me smarter than you, entrepreneur!"

Second, consider whether or not the concept is worth pursuing at your present company.

- Is there someone in the organization who can be trusted help you shape up your plan so it can be re-presented?

- Is there an open door policy further up the food chain? A Department of Last Resort? Or would running an end-around just be a short cut to getting yourself a pink slip?

- Are there other reasons you've been looking elsewhere, and this most recent affront is feeling like the last straw? Perhaps it even seems that the stars are aligning that way, since recruiters have been calling you day and night with tempting offers.

Finally, make your decision, and follow your path.

- Is there enough potential commercial value and growth potential to enable you to attract seed capital?

- Can you build your own prototype during your off hours? Land a space in a business incubator? Get a grant?

- Are you sure you would not be violating any obligations to your present company? Would a top plaintiff's attorney agree with you?

If you're not confident in your ability to make it happen on your own, it's OK to just let it go. But you really should give some thought to finding a more collegial work environment!

Innovation is precious, and often fragile. Whatever you do, don't let yourself be the one who put the 'no' in innovation!

@DrJanice: If you are working for yourself, you need to sell. You are, aren't you? #justasking

More on my daughter, as well as on sales. I have a son too, but he's much more like me so he's easier to deal with, but harder to get funny about.

Like It or Not: You're in Sales!

Fifteen years ago, my daughter worked for a company that was swallowed up in one of those merger deals where the people on the upside of the power curve got to call all the shots. Her group was given the golden opportunity to pull up stakes and move halfway across the continent. At the time, she had only been in the workforce for a few years, and she had a lot more ability than had ever been exercised in that job anyway, so she opted out.

Those of you who are parents know what a thrill it can be when your grown children ask for advice, especially so soon after you have recovered from their adolescence. When she called for an opinion about the kind of job she should look for next, I dropped everything to give it serious consideration.

I contemplated the future of this intense young woman who calls me mom. She's a five foot dynamo with a head full of wild red curls on the outside, and equally wild and colorful feelings inside. She's also a loyal friend and has the most caring heart I know. But in seconds, I was caught up in the ramifications of developing markets, industrial shifts, and new technologies that might impact her future. I finally said, "You make such an impact on people, you should be in sales." First mistake: Never say 'you should' to a child who has been getting a regular paycheck. Second mistake: Never underestimate the extent of negative association that many people have for salespeople and selling.

Let's just say that the consultation got off to a rocky start.

Sales, Marketing, and Business Development are often used interchangeably these days, and to be sure, there can be some overlap. In smaller companies, where people are more likely to have some input into their job title, the word sales doesn't always appear on the business card even when 95%+ of the job is exactly that. Really, are you fooled when you get a cold call from the Director of Marketing at ABC Office Supply? I didn't think so, but it makes the point: even some professional salespeople don't want to own up to what they do for a living.

Had I given it more thought, I would have taken care in responding to my offspring. But it got me to wondering. By whatever term you call it, what makes a good salesperson? The answer depends on what's for sale:

- Is it something that is sold in abstract terms like "What would it mean to you if...?" My iPad may look like a trendy toy to you, but to me, it transcends time and space and has totally changed the way I do my job.

- Is it something that is purely practical and money- or time-saving? Back when I was the President of a sheet metal manufacturing company, if someone could show me how their press brake could reduce waste by 5% while increasing productivity by 15%+, with an ROI under 12 months, they would be pocketing their commission in no time flat.

- Or is it something that lifts spirits and makes people feel they are doing good things in the world? Think about all the things you buy that fall into this category: memberships, sponsorships, lessons, or entertainment.

Attempting to get back on track with my daughter, I pointed out that she had been very effective in selling me on the items in that last group. What could be wrong with that? Her answer was short, and not very sweet. "Mom, that's not selling. *Selling* is about getting people to buy things they don't need."

Oh dear, I thought. She's a very mainstream GenXer. This doesn't bode well for the sales profession. But I was not about to give up. I raised her to be a good listener so I donned my official HR Guru chapeau, and gravely intoned my three rules for ethical sales success:

1. Believe in what you are selling, whether it's an idea, a technology, or an imprinted pen. If you don't use it, why should I? When your eyes sparkle as you talk about it, you make me want to buy it, do it, or be part of it. Excitement engenders more excitement, whether or not I have long desired exactly what you are selling.

2. Express your self-confidence, but nicely. No one likes a smarty-pants. If you don't think you have enough, then go find it or find a way to develop some. Start small, with something you know reasonably well. Influencing other people is really the most natural form of leadership — even if it doesn't come naturally.

3. Take the risk that someone will say no to you. What will happen if someone turns you down? Nothing. The world keeps on spinning. If you won't get into the game, how will you know if you're a winner?

Okay, I got a little buy-in at this point, but I wasn't closing the deal. So I resorted to something that occasionally worked during preadolescent shopping trips: the 'try-it-on-you-don't-have-to-take-it-home' approach. I got very, very quiet for a few moments and then said, "You know, you are a seller of dreams, of caring, of love and light." What could she do? She knew I was right and gave a nearly imperceptible little nod that announced itself quite readily to my maternal eye. Coming in for the kill, I smiled and asked, "Can't you sell just one more thing?"

I had made the point for her, and oddly enough, for myself as well, that when you like and believe in something, you can sell it effectively. So at work, no matter whether you answer the phone, interview vendors, recruit new customers, or drive a delivery truck, you are selling yourself, and your company, all day, every day.

Here are a few points that will help you make the most of it:

- Be as nice to yourself as you are to other people. Treat yourself as your own best customer and it will show in everything you do.

- Take your time with people and treat them as if they are your only concern at the moment. Pay special attention to what is important to each one and take an interest in it. Focus on your customer and let your product take care of itself.

- Make each person feel special. Small courtesies will go a long way, so unless you have a perfect memory, make notes after each encounter so you can personalize the next one.

- Listen carefully to current and potential customers. If you can find their pain points, you'll be able find the right antidote for what ails them.

- Encourage your customers to supersize their dreams. Let their fantasies soar, then show them how your product or service will help them get there. And remember, you won't be very good at getting other people to do this if you don't have some big dreams of your own!

In case you are wondering about my daughter, here's what happened. She went to work as a customer service rep for a medical supplies company, and she enjoys her work! She provides loving care by helping customers make choices that fit their needs and their budgets, and she's great at this because she knows exactly which products will make the person's life a little easier. And although she doesn't really think of it this way, she is constantly upselling and cross-selling in ways that benefit both her customers and her company. She also services heath care providers, and since they pass on the good word in their circles, she develops new commercial business without even thinking about it.

I'm happy because I see her doing what she does well. Her employer is happy because the customers are loyal, and sales are rising. She's happy because she knows she's helping people, and our relationship is better than ever because I never, ever, say she is in sales.

@DrJanice: Imagine a workforce where everyone is a great team player! #Teamability

My mother was very ill and had advanced dementia, but she liked to reminisce about her childhood. It got me thinking about mine. She used to call me Mary, Mary, Quite Contrary when I wouldn't follow her wishes. Later in life, I learned that it was not such a bad thing to be a contrarian, so I got some mentoring to be better at it and passed on what I learned.

Effective Contrariness: How Does Your Garden Grow?

I wasn't the most compliant child and my mother often reminded me of that by reciting, "Mary, Mary, quite contrary, how does your garden grow?" I will confess now, I wasn't much of a gardener either. My five-year-old standards were based on picture books of life on a farm, far from the urban New York City of the time, but my garden was a package of radish seeds from the gift shop at the Brooklyn Botanical Gardens, lovingly placed in a wooden cheese box filled with what we called "dirt." ("Dirt" was a kind of urban soil purloined from the local park with a small pail and shovel.) Even the most non-contrary of thoughts could not turn the few green sprouts and occasional red root into Eden, but of course as a five year old, I assumed it was my contrariness that was causing the lack of lush vegetation on my window sill. I outgrew the feeling of being a failure at farming as soon as my interests turned elsewhere, but not the feeling that somehow, if I could only lose just a bit of that contrariness, that something magical would happen.

I didn't think about it again until I was running the HR department of a company with a few hundred employees. They made active lifestyle-related products, so the majority of those employees were young people, both male and female, and the dress code, especially to my very maternal eyes appeared to be wear what you slept and/or did your morning workout in (for the young men) or wear the least you possibly can considering we keep the thermostat at 68° (for the young women). Is it any surprise there were a dozen active sexual harassment cases? I needed to get that garden weeded, and fast.

HR people in organizations that size are generally charged with fixing the smaller problems, the day to day issues that gum up the works, while the long range planning and orders for the day come down from the top. That's been the historical value of HR and in most organizations that's still the way it is. Despite HR's interest in becoming more of a strategic partner and having a seat at the corporate management table, it's happening only in companies where senior management has bought into the human infrastructure model.

There wasn't much buy-in from management. In fact, most of the cases involved less-than-stellar management behavior. (I won't go into detail here. If you are reading this, you've likely seen worse in your career.) But I didn't really notice much because I was on a mission. The garden couldn't possibly be flourishing with all those threats of judicial thunder and lightening and something needed to be done. I needed all the contrariness I could muster.

The funny thing was, the rest of the nursery rhyme seemed to be working fine. There were silver bells and cockle shells and pretty maids all in a row, or at least in nicely aligned cubicles in the customer service department. And they were used to being treated like the flowers in a garden – admired for how they looked, pruned when they got out of line and not expected to last more than the current season.

I discovered that the head of customer service was actually quite contrary herself, and her young blossoms loved her for it. She went to bat for them, carefully choosing where she would make her impact. She was an expert in the first rule of contrariness: start small. She had no large aspirations for major organizational revolution but I learned a lot from her. She made the most miniscule of changes, generally too small for anyone in upper management to notice (or object to), but always with the complete approval and support of HR. I rationalized that these were such small changes they would never be of concern to upper management so why bother telling them. Operating on the assumption that it's easier to ask for forgiveness than permission, we made a series of imperceptible changes that eventually added up to decreased turnover and increased employee satisfaction.

Thinking about that time from my perspective now, almost twenty years later, I wonder if successful HR leaders in less-than-optimal organizations are more contrary than most other people. I do know that it takes a certain level of contrariness to express those responsible opposing viewpoints that senior management often forgets can bring value to their decision making process. In fact, what we call contrary depends on where we're standing. To the boss, you might be contrary, but what if you were regarded instead as being a contributor of a unique, different-from-the-boss's viewpoint? That certainly changes the picture. There may be value in everyone wearing the company logo on their uniform, but does that mean the boss wants and, more importantly, benefits from uniform minds?

My experience coaching HR people has taught me that there are a goodly number who prefer to be seen as being contrary, in a positive way. They pride themselves on speaking the truth, empowering themselves and their people, and keeping the garden neatly weeded and well nurtured. I don't have the definitive answers, but I can offer some advice on becoming better at what I'd like to call *Effective Contrariness*.

- Start with small changes and make sure the people who will benefit from them know you are doing it because you care about them.

- You don't have to give people the HR theory or a strategic plan to back up what you're doing. It's enough that you tell them you're doing it because it's the right thing to do.

- You don't need to get immediate credit for doing it, but keep your documentation handy. At the first sign of success, measured by however they measure these things in your organization, write it up and distribute it. Remember to push the right buttons for the right people in the right way – at the right time.

- Your small actions can have huge consequences, so make sure you are acting in alignment with the vision or ethical system that nurtures you and makes you feel as if you are reaching for the highest stars.

- Remember, you have enormous power that cannot be taken away. It's like a lush garden right inside you, but if it's not cared for, it will wither. All it needs to grow is the sunlight of your vision, the rain of your caring for other people, the fertile imagination of your mind and the weeding of your potential actions.

I should add a postscript here for those aficionados of the real meaning behind nursery rhymes. (If you are wondering, I did not learn this part from my mother. It was pointed out to me by a truly effective HR person working in a dysfunctional organization that shall remain nameless. This person will probably get the world's first Ph.D. in Effective Contrariness.)

The Mary in the rhyme allegedly refers to Mary Tudor (aka Bloody Mary), daughter of King Henry VIII, who preemptively kept her religious, political opposition to a minimum with a variety of torture and murder devices, notably silver bells (thumbscrews), cockle shells (similar to the silver bells but applied to a much more delicate region of her victims' bodies) and pretty maids (iron maidens, a kind of a coffin with strategically placed daggers inside the walls).

Those are pretty gruesome images, but think about the talk we often hear in business environments. Has someone in your organization, said 'heads will roll' lately, while creatively attempting to affix blame? Do contracts get signed after someone 'puts the screws on' or 'nails them to the wall'?

HR is often viewed as the handmaiden of upper management, there to insulate the boss from potential uprisings in the garden. That's why Catbert (the Evil HR Director in Scott Adams' Dilbert cartoon) is Evil and the Boss merely pointy-haired. (If you don't get Dilbert in your daily newspaper, or even if you do, go to www.dilbert.com and get your daily fix. Anything you've missed in your own experience can be learned there.) The contrariness you value is really your ability to think for yourself, not your ability to figure out clever ways to do what the boss wants, but that you know will be bad, in the long run, for the company, the people, and you.

That's the true value of Effective Contrariness.

@DrJanice: Respect people for what they bring to the table. Let them fulfill their mission in life.

Details, details. Most people notice some, some people notice most. A few people notice every detail. I hardly notice any. That could make me an anti-detail snob, but no, I've always been fascinated by detail people so I observed them until I got their big picture.

Everyone Notices Something

It's either God or the devil that's in the details, depending on who you ask, but it's clear that everyone's got an opinion on details and their importance. I used to think that only some very special people are detail-oriented just like it reads on their resumes, but I've got it figured out now. We're all detail oriented. It's just that the details we notice aren't necessarily the same ones the next guy notices.

There are two aspects to details. The first is where you tend to focus. The second is to what extent you actually act on what you notice. Some people use their details to plan, plan, plan – sometimes to the extent that they get into the endless loop that's been called analysis paralysis. Others don't even realize they've noticed anything till they catch themselves acting on it, and sometimes not even then. Where's the happy medium? It's at the place where you know what you notice, notice it more fully, and can figure out how to use what you notice to get something done, whether you do it yourself or are managing other people who are doing the actual work.

The key questions to ask are is where do I tend to focus? What details do I notice and use the most in my everyday life? What do I pay the most attention to? These are probably quite similar whether you are at work or at home, but be sure to consider both environments, especially if your home and work life diverge considerably. The key to improving your attention to details is to improve the one area you're best at and let the other areas alone for now. The amazing thing is that as you improve that one, the others will also improve, and with no wasted effort.

Some people focus on details that involve time. The strongest of this group are rarely late for appointments (unless they want to be) and they are the world's consummate planners. They're rarely caught short on anything. At their best, they make meticulous lists and keep detailed calendars. They focus on the longer-term details, so they make good project planners, whether that's building a bridge, managing a software development initiative, or planning a party.

Other people focus on details that involve space. They are much more observant of their immediate environment than those who focus on time, so they tend to think of themselves as detail oriented, unlike people in the first group who find it much easier to overlook the mundane, such as having placemats that match. Those who notice space details have an eye for proportion and tend to get pictures to hang straight and desks, even overused ones, look organized.

The third group tends to focus on the details that involve value. Whether they notice what would affect shareholder value or their own paycheck, their focus is on value. This focus may also be directed toward spiritual values, ethics, entrepreneurship, or the initial development of ideas, products, and services that inspire others.

So in which dimension and to what extent do you tend to notice things? And, more important, how can you improve your powers of observation? Here are some tips.

For the time-oriented:

- Write out your plans. For instance, if you want to give your career a booster shot, detail your timeline, paying special attention to the things you will need from other people (references, introductions, etc.) to get where you want to go.

- Don't forget that at some point it is necessary for the planning to stop and it becomes necessary for implementation to begin. You will never be perfectly prepared for anything.

- Remember that time is relative. A few minutes sitting on a hot stove is a LOT longer than a few minutes kissing the one you love.

- No matter how much you plan, luck plays a part in success, too. If it goes against you, allow yourself to relax and recover and then try again.

- Get other points of view to help your planning. As the Chinese proverb goes, "Scholars planning a rebellion could never succeed."

For the space-oriented:

- Organize your tasks visually, in any form that makes sense to you. Use the colors you associate with successful action and be sure you really like the way it looks before you put it into use. For instance, if you are trying to organize the details of your interview wardrobe, take digital photos of complete outfits you like and print them so if something is at the cleaners you have additional choices right at hand. (This also works for suitcase organization on business and pleasure trips.)

- Rely heavily on what *you* consider important and don't worry so much about what others may consider important. You will get further.

- Decide which battles are worth fighting. Don't throw your efforts into trying to succeed everywhere: you can't do it. You will arrange things in areas or domains. Put your efforts into those domains where you have the greatest chances of success. As Henry Ford said, "Failure is the opportunity to begin again, more intelligently."

- Your greatest strength is to act like a centipede and walk on a hundred legs. If one or two run into trouble, you still have a lot more that are working. You have so many areas that are strong, you can afford to have a few that aren't.

- Organize your work into areas and as much as possible devote your greatest effort to those areas that you love. It will help you build up your strengths so much that they will compensate for your weak areas.

For the value-oriented:

- Take an inventory of your values by writing your own mission statement. Think about how you want to live, how you want to be remembered, and what dreams you want to see fulfilled. It can be short or long, complex or simple, but be sure that it reflects your ideals.

- Don't orient yourself to a scarcity approach. The universe will provide. The environment tends to manifest according to your expectations.

- The problems you encounter can have a hidden value to you. As John Foster Dulles said, "The measure of success is not whether you have a tough problem to deal with, but whether it's the same problem you had last year." You can use this concept to measure your real progress. If you are encountering new problems, you are making progress toward your goals.

- Use your skills to determine the real value of your opportunities. Pursuing an opportunity that wastes your time and energy can cost a great deal but passing up an opportunity that has hidden value can cost a great deal more.

- Understand what you value. Regardless of what you seem to value, what you really value is what you are willing to risk.

@DrJanice: My favorite method of facilitation is getting out of the way. #leadership #teamwork

Part 2: Teams & Teamwork

Many years ago I read an article that said that most people's strongest frustration at work was their idiot boss. I vowed then that I would never be an idiot boss. Then I realized that I already had that covered when I'd vowed not to be an idiot mother so many years earlier.

Yes, I have broken both vows. And repented.

But it is much easier as a CEO than it was as a young mother, because I now have a fabulous, coherent team, and I know I have to work very hard to be worthy. They each contribute in their own special way, but they have one thing in common:

They are my early warning system for idiocy. For this, I treasure them.

@DrJanice: Music is what happens between the notes. Teaming is what happens between the people. #teamwork

When we started the company there were so few of us that you could hardly call us a team. That's when I realized that sometimes the most important team members aren't the ones you pay. They're the ones who pay you.

Are Your Customers On Your Team?

For the start up, every person and every advisor you need to hire represents a critical commitment of the company's available time and cash. In essence, you trade those resources for the knowledge and skill (intellectual assets), contacts (social capital), and the pure energy, ideas, and actions you expect that person to bring to your budding organization.

But what if you could get some of same resources without having to give up any of your precious start-up funds?

You can if you put your customers – and those you'd like to have as customers – on your team! Here are three ways to start:

1. Stop thinking of customers as 'them'. Customers are stakeholders who can help you move and shape your vision. Try posing a provocative question that will trigger thoughtful responses. For instance, my company created a completely new way to predict how people perform in teams, but we were struggling to find a way to properly present it. So I started asking, "Why do people say they want team players, and then hire people who aren't?" Instant reaction! We not only got some great feedback, but some of our customers even went out and recruited other customers for us!

When a company is in the early stages of development, input from vision-oriented people can be especially valuable, and vision people are intrigued by big picture questions. They'll probably give you good advice, so make sure you let them know how you've used it.

2. Add some customers to the marketing R&D team. Find a low risk way if you can, to get them engaged in using your product in a way that will deliver real business value. If you find out they have a problem that your product can solve, let them apply your solution (at least once) at no charge. We learned pretty quickly that if we gave people enough product to use for one solution, they would experience the value of a pre-hire positive I.D. on real team players, and it would bring them back for more.

3. Give someone a reason to feel good! It was Benjamin Franklin who said, "If you want to make a friend, ask a favor." Good team players actually LIKE to help others out. Whether you need a source of information, a second opinion, a pep talk, or some help getting something done but no resources to pay for it, there's probably someone who will take on that job and be happy to share with you what they've found. But not until you ask! Just be sure to let them know how valuable their input is and be very clear in letting them know that when they need your help for something, you will give it gladly. You'll end up just a little bit closer to someone who now feels they have a stake in your success. Remember, people who are good at finding things you need are also good at finding people who need exactly what you are selling.

So how's business? How's your team? Are you working with them…or without them?

@DrJanice: Align recognition with how the person sees themself as contributing. Everything else will go over their head.

I like the idea of simple systems. They're easier to keep unbiased, you don't have to keep adjusting them, and you're never far from successfully completing them.

Three Questions for Performance Management

Ask any manager about their least favorite tasks, and more than likely they'll put performance evaluations at or near the top of the list.

Why? Lots of reasons, not the least of which is the 'Gotcha!': an assumption that you need to find something deficient in each staff member, and come up with a prescription for fixing it, thereby improving performance. All too often, you're going to find something that the person thinks they are doing very well (and they may be right), or something they have no interest in doing better. At worst, you're expected to assign tasks or reassign job responsibilities to develop one person's undesired something, which may well be a task or a job that someone else on your team really enjoys (or would enjoy) doing! Here's an even better approach. Just ask these three questions:

- Are you doing enough of what you like?

- Are you doing too much of what you don't like?

- What can we do to change these things and make them better?

If someone isn't doing enough of what they really like, they are probably:

(a) in the wrong job,
(b) looking for another job,
(c) not very productive, or
(d) all of the above!

If someone on your team is doing too much of what they don't like, the problem may not reside in the individual, but rather, in the team. The causes: a team that is missing people with key needed Roles; the team's vision, mission, or goals have not been communicated clearly enough; or, there is less-than-optimal coherence on the team.

The good news is that you can change these conditions and make the team work better for everyone.

Start with Teamability reports for the whole team, yourself included. Then compare who you have (the Roles) with what you need (the right Roles for the team's mission). Finally, look at what needs to be done, figure which person is best prepared (by Role) to achieve each need, and confirm with people that they have the right tools – and teammates – to do their job better.

The whole point of performance evaluation is to improve performance. Try this approach and the improvement will be obvious to management, to your staff, and to you!

(You'll learn more about the concepts of Teamability in the third section of this book.)

@DrJanice: You don't have to be out front to lead. #PM

Project managers who attend our course in Teamability come from diverse organizations in all parts of the world. What they have in common is the desire to learn new and better ways to deal with some of the challenges that are intrinsic to project management. These include having a great deal of responsibility, and often not nearly enough authority to drive effective performance; working with cross-functional teams in environments where the various functions represented are at odds; and dealing with people who have been assigned to their team, but who are not necessarily prepared for – or supportive of – the mission, or the job responsibilities that they encounter. But PMs also have the ability to ask questions and learn new applications, so I was delighted when I received a transcript of recently asked questions.

The Project Manager Project

I'm going to answer two of the questions that were especially energizing to me, including some thoughts on how PMs can empower themselves to organize the people, processes, and controls that will enable them to deliver successful projects by reducing stress, developing team synergy, and improving overall team performance.

Q: *How do we get 100% true team players? Doesn't it depend on the company, the culture, the favoritism levels, number of years in the company, true diversity levels, business leaders' professional training levels, and the big one - communication - because being a good communicator doesn't mean you are a good team player?*

A: Having 100% true team players is a beautiful goal, and Teamability® provides the means to get you there. However, because of the various obstacles you mentioned, it's very likely to be a long-term effort. So instead, let's focus on the ways that Teamability can help Project Managers achieve a critically important near term goal: working with team members more effectively, helping them collaborate more readily, and producing the kind of business results that will raise the value and visibility of successful teaming.

Here are three steps in that direction:

First, for each person on the team, try to align job responsibilities with the way in which that person wishes to serve their team (their Role, as identified by Teamability). Since many people spend every day doing work that doesn't satisfy (or even connect with) their inner need to serve a specific type of organizational need, any work that actually DOES fulfill that desire will quickly be perceived as exciting and invigorating.

Second, you want to make sure that people who will be encountering the most resistance, tackling the hardest problems, and/or feeling the most time pressure, are also the most coherent members of the team (something else Teamability measures). Less coherent people can be excellent contributors, and good team players, but they are also more susceptible to stress, and as we all know, people who are feeling a great deal of stress are generally not at their best.

Finally – and this can be the easiest or hardest, depending on those cultural and favoritism factors you mentioned – you need to promote a culture of respect, trust, and belief in working together as a team. This effort will be greatly enhanced if you can apply the principle that respect and appreciation is best delivered in a way that a person is most likely to internalize it. This, too, will align with their Role. (Information about a free online course in the use of Teamability is available at http://bit.ly/TmbtyCrs and, by the way, it is eligible for four PMI Category B credits.)

Here's the other question that got to me. And it's not just for PMs.

Q: *We have one team player that is a bully, and our team is very small. We don't want to work with him so how do the rest of us deal with him?*

A: Bullying behavior is often rooted in fear. People who bully others are dealing with their fear in ways that may make them feel better, but are (at minimum) ineffective, and (more likely) damaging to team performance. The more stress there is in the environment, the worse this kind of behavior can get. Consequently, arranging an occasional stress break for the team is a valuable practice, but try to include the bully. Even just a shared laugh is a great stress breaker, which is why so many project teams enjoy gallows humor! Once you get the bully laughing, bullying tends to subside, at least for a little while.

Here's another little trick. Take note of the degree of friendliness the bully is exhibiting. When you are dealing with him or her, don't be even one little bit friendlier than that. (Don't be nasty; just go cool/neutral. If you are naturally very friendly and smiling, this may be very hard for you!) At the same time, pretend you have very little power (which, paradoxically, is just about the most powerful thing you can do in this situation!) and tell him or her you have no answers. When the bully tries to tell you what to do, ask for more, and more, and more details. Sooner or later, he or she will run out of answers and probably tell you to go figure it out yourself. And that is really what you want, isn't it?

The key to bully handling is the avoidance of any kind of a power struggle. If you can do this, while practicing the appropriate respect and keeping the bully focused on job responsibilities, the bully's fear will subside and the general tone of his/her behavior will improve, at least for as long as the stress level remains relatively low.

This same strategy is also effective with know-it-all people, and with those who seem to want everyone else to be dependent on them.

A final note: sometimes the best you can do is just not make it worse. If you do that, please congratulate yourself!

@DrJanice: Leader or not, you are part of your team. If you had a choice, would you want to be on the #team you run?

I wasn't surprised when I saw these numbers because they were so consistent with what people were talking about. It seemed like everyone I met was open to a new opportunity. A deeper dive with some of them produced these thoughts.

Here Today, Team Tomorrow

At the end of 2009, the experts at Right Management surveyed more than 900 workers in North America, asking a seemingly innocuous question: "Do you plan to pursue new job opportunities as the economy improves in 2010?"

These were the responses

- 60% said they intend to leave in 2010

- 21% said they might, so they're networking

- 6% said it wasn't likely, but they have an updated resume

- And only 13% stated their intention is to stay in their present job

You can look at this data in two contexts.

First, you can think of what it means on the employee level and glean some pretty useful plans. You can do the math and realize you might be needing to replace up to 87% of your workforce. You can hire another recruiter – or ten. You can change your comp and incentive plans to try to keep your mission–critical people. You can even start cross training, internship, mentoring, engagement, and similar programs.

Or, for something completely different, you can think about your workforce as a human infrastructure. How could it have become so fragile? How can it be restored? What have we been missing? How can we avoid repeating the same mistakes?

Obviously something has been missing, and there's a good chance that you need to learn the 'new math' of valuing people's performance in teams. And to avoid making the same mistakes, get answers to these questions before you launch a massive recruiting drive:

- What do we really need to accomplish: adding more people, or building a sustainable human infrastructure?

- If it's true that people leave managers, not companies, what's the best way to identify and support managers who naturally get people to stick around, and how can we replicate their success?

- Are we using measurements that were designed to identify teaming characteristics and to solve team performance problems? If not, why not?

- Have we structured our teams correctly, ensuring that the teaming characteristics of the people are a good fit to the functional mission of the team?

And finally:

- What's our strategy for identifying and dealing the people who just don't fit – never have and never will?

Could it be that you never had the right people on the bus in the first place?

@DrJanice: My imperfection means I need your perfection in that area. #justsaying

I'm not perfect. Not even close. And I think that's why most of the time I'm happy. But I still had to check up on myself to know if I'd bought into the myth of the perfect leader.

Perfection is Highly Overrated. How About Just Being You?

Leadership isn't easy, but there are a lot of people who can tell you how it's done! You can find about 69,000 of them on Amazon.com. Read a few, and soon you will be ready for the fitting of your halo and wings.

Last year I answered a question about leadership on Quora. com. I have a special place in my heart for this website. The questions that people ask and answer there can range from tough to touching. The question I picked was, What are the top 10 interpersonal skills found in great leaders? It was irresistible because I've met a lot of people who seem to believe that a team is only as good as its leader, and that is just not so!

Here's my Top 10:

1. They are team players.

2. They are coherent (neither rigid nor diffuse) in all their interactions with others.

3. Depending on what they are leading, they are either highly inspirational, in which case people are drawn to follow them and their vision, or they are excellent at shepherding people toward the goal. Occasionally you find people who are good at both.

4. They take initiative, especially in innovation companies – they seize the moment, and go for the opportunity.

5. They clearly get that other people have a point of view that may not be an exact mirror of theirs. (They might not like it, but they definitely get it.)

6. They aren't consumed by greed. Their ambition and desire to win extends to their team, organization, stakeholders, and especially their customers.

7. They aren't know-it-alls, even though they are generally smart.

8. They know how to be able to depend on other people – their trust is highly desired and valued.

9. They respect all living things. (That includes silicon-based life forms – the technology that runs the company.)

10. They openly express their faith in their team, that together they can achieve the vision.

After I posted it, I had to ask myself if I was only feeding into the perfection myth, but they checked out OK, especially #7 & #8.

Leaders need to acknowledge their imperfections, and that is actually the perfect team's scenario. Every thing you do not do well calls for someone on your team who does do it well, and who loves having the opportunity. This gives the team, as an entity in and of itself, a much greater chance of being perfect than a 'perfect' leader ever could, or should.

No, leadership is not a formula, or a style, or a canon. Neither can it be adequately described as a series of traits or bits and pieces of experience. Leadership is intertwined with situational context, and thus leadership is a team sport. In the end, all that matters is that, collectively, your team is pulling together to achieve its mission.

There is a way to describe what any team needs, in terms of the people who are attracted to fill those needs. Each has a Role. Not a 'role' – like a job title or a set of responsibilities – but

Role in the language of Teamability: the manner or mode in which a given person seeks to make meaningful contributions to meet team needs.

When you understand that you cannot do all of these things well, you may feel angry, or cheated, or sad in your imperfection. Or, you may suddenly realize that your moments of greatest joy and fulfillment have come when you were entirely immersed in contributions that were aligned with Your Role – and that in those moments, you were grateful for the others on your team who were also experiencing joy in performing their own life's mission. When people and teams are functioning this way, they generate tremendous positive synergy and performance, producing real business value for an organization.

@DrJanice: Things that have meaning are done by teams. It's an illusion that we're so powerful that we accomplish in a vacuum. #teamwork

Four eyes are better than two; two heads are better than one. When you have someone who serves in ways that you don't, you have the possibility to raise the power of the parallax. But it is not easy to draw the distinction between what is of value and what is not unless you know that you are talking about the same thing.

The Power of Parallax

A while ago, I shared a rather dense article about sub-nuclear physics with Jack (TGI's co-founder, Dr. Jack Gerber), and then we connected on Skype. I said, you know, this is what we were talking about fifteen years ago. He agreed, saying he'd always meant to write it up. (We work that way. He's a Curator of the most brilliant sort, and he knows how to pull information together in exactly the right way. Then I inject the vision and launch it into the future.)

The following day, via email, he mentioned new thoughts on the subject, and wanted to speak with me before he started writing. (This is a great thing about having such a seasoned Curator on the team. He can access huge amounts of knowledge, so he checks to be sure that he is delivering the specific bits you asked for.) I was really eager to hear him because I'd had a few new thoughts myself.

We often speak by phone as I'm walking home at the end of the office day (aka, the beginning of my night shift – take your choice.) This time, Jack jumped on the topic so suddenly that I was momentarily confused. I had been expecting a next step in our prior conversation, but he seemed to be on a completely unrelated path. Or was I just not thinking straight?

Nothing is quite as scary as thinking you're not thinking straight. But never one to panic, I stopped making judgments and just listened a little harder. Soon I realized that although we were still on the subject of the article, we had each come away from it with a totally different take on why it was important and relevant to our work!

There are three ways that people respond to this sort of disjoint. First, they may become annoyed, or even angry. Second, they may get curious and just ask. Third, they may get connected at a higher level. It isn't that one way is inherently better or worse. They're just different — and here's what you can learn from this:

If you get annoyed, that's just evidence that you don't like your vision tampered with. The upside is you hold your own in a disagreement. The downside might be that you miss a lot of value coming from your opponent.

If you get curious and wonder where the other person is coming from, make sure that after you ask the question you wait around for their answer. You can benefit a lot that way, even if what you get isn't what you thought you wanted to know.

While it sounds like getting connected should be the right answer, it isn't always. Just going along to get along deprives you of having your own voice in the matter, and also deprives the other person of hearing it. Connecting in parallax is much more effective.

Here's what I mean by connecting in parallax. A person's two eyes work together in seeing the world from slightly different points of view, and this enables the brain to perceive depth by putting the two views together. Depth perception doesn't exist before the two views merge into the third collective view.

So how do you apply this to your work?

First, remember to simply listen. And to listen simply. That means listening without the distractions of your environment, your electronics, and your own thoughts.

Then try to give your colleague total respect by closing your own 'eye' and viewing the interaction completely and solely through theirs. The value of this exercise can be enhanced when you understand their Role and how to respect it. With some practice and care, you may learn to connect very deeply for a time.

Finally, take time to *appreciate* their contribution before *modifying* it with your own. It will help you remember why you listened to them in the first place.

If you are curious about what happened next with Jack and me, I'll tell you. We discovered that he had made one discovery, and I had made another. But most importantly, through the power of parallax, both of them became <u>ours</u>.

@DrJanice: People who are intimidating are usually full of fear. Try relaxing them. #leadership

Most people shy away from situations that make them fearful. I don't. Sometimes I think I'm just not smart enough to leave well enough alone. But when you're trying to bring a disruptive inno-vation to the world, you need to plug right through those reservations and just do it. Whatever 'it' is. In this case it was launching a project on Indiegogo, which we named Trepability. So of course, like buying a bag to go with new shoes, I just had to start the blog. And the story was picked up by Forbes.com. You can read it here: http://bit.ly/ForbesT410K

What's Your Fear Factor?

I started a new blog one day. It was for an audience I hadn't said much to yet. I called it Trepability – think Teamability for entre-preneurs. It was for treps – a.k.a. entrepreneurs – and the people who love them. And while getting the word out, I learned that not everyone knows what a trep is. Even some entrepreneurs.

The most interesting thread in the comments I got from people was that they associated trep with trepidation.

Let me distinguish those two words with a bit more precision.

Trep: an entrepreneur, one who incites, energizes, and/or leads an enterprise into existence, generally with great initiative and high tolerance for risk. My kinda people.

Trepidation: tremulous fear, alarm, or agitation; perturbation. Or as some may be wont to define it, scared s**tless.

These are, in fact, mutually exclusive terms.

Being a trepidation-less trep doesn't ensure you'll be a successful one, but it certainly doesn't hurt. And it's not a bad idea to know where you stand. Here's my user-friendly trep[idation] test. Just read the three choices and decide which applies most to you.

a) The only thing I can really focus on is fear.

b) I totally ignore fear.

c) It's there, but so what?

That wasn't too hard, was it? (If you are still vacillating, your answer is probably a).

And here's your Fear Factor:

If you chose a), you aren't focusing, you're obsessing. Getting caught in the cycle of fearful rumination is incredibly bad for innovation.

If you chose b), you're missing the kind of awareness that is essential for effectively delegating the handling of risk to someone who can worry without getting stuck, and can actually do something about it. And while risk might not kill you, you may be taking unnecessary chances without a safety net.

If you chose c), you've got the awareness that fear needs to be managed, just not by you. You don't want anything to distract you from what only you can do, so you trust the right person to make sure the roof stays over your head and there are plenty of ramen noodles in the supply closet.

Trepidation isn't going away. Whether you're a trep or not, fear is built in to our lives. But with the right team, we can free ourselves to fly!

@DrJanice: You want #teamwork, first stop lying to employees.

This was written after my neighbor's son didn't get hired after taking an 'honesty test'. Honestly, I have no idea what the people at this company thought they were doing.

The Problem of Corporate Theft

I got a call the other day, one of those conversations that begin, "You know about this stuff. What can I do?" It was Ron, a nice guy I once met at a nice neighbor's house. His younger brother, Carl, had just applied for a job with a large company and didn't get hired after all the signals were pointing positive: he's a perfect match for his experience level, he knows a lot of people who work there and likes them so he'll fit right in and he had great interviews that ended with strong handshakes all around. Then he was sent to the HR department to fill out some forms and that was the end. The 'thanks but no thanks' letter had just come in the mail.

I got Carl on the phone, asked him enough questions about those forms to figure out that one was an honesty test and made the diagnosis in a flash. Sounded to me like a case of Corporate Theft Phobia. I've been seeing a lot of it recently.

The problem of corporate theft is usually attributed to employees' bad behavior. That's true, and it's a difficult, persistent, expensive problem. There are two methods that companies use to deal with it. Unfortunately, neither of them works very well. The first, most obvious approach is not to hire employees who will steal. There are assessments that purport to select for honesty, but most any dishonest Psych 101 student can learn to beat them. Also, they don't distinguish very well between people who will take a half empty disposable pen home with them and those who will highjack your truck and fence the contents.

There is another problem with these tests. Since most people will steal something (more likely the pen) given the proper circumstances and motivation, if the company only hires honest employees they tend to be left with very few people to hire. As the job market grows, this will become an even more serious problem. As it is, there are many industries where the same people get recycled, working for first one company then another.

The more common method is the deterrent approach, which centers on the threat of disciplinary action. It works well if all of its three components are present. First, your people have to know something bad will happen if they steal. Second, your people need to believe it will happen to them, that is, if they steal, they will be caught and punished. Third, your people have to care about getting fired. But that's the problem with deterrents. It is very rare that all three conditions are present. Prisons are filled with people who either never thought or believed they would be caught, or just didn't care at the time.

And some people don't care about being fired. They even prefer it, especially if they have worked long enough to qualify for unemployment benefits. The problem is, many employers will ignore the fact that the person was fired for cause and won't challenge the benefits award. It's hard when you pride yourself on being a nice guy.

The treatment of Corporate Theft Phobia is tough. First, it makes sense to define theft as being the taking of something more valuable than the half used disposable pen. Unless you have a very special situation, it will be easier if you accept that some theft is inevitable and your goal should be to cut it to a minimum rather than try, unsuccessfully, to eliminate it completely.

Here are some action steps you can take to protect your business.

Start with a security assessment that identifies your organization's vulnerabilities. This assessment should include an internal audit of finances, information technology and other critical systems.

Second, forgo traditional honesty tests, which often weed out excellent employees and allow in people who are dishonest, but are sophisticated enough to fool the testers. If you're going to use an assessment, use one that's been customized to specifically address your organization's vulnerabilities but make sure that it doesn't discriminate on the basis of any factor such as race or gender. And remember that even though past behavior is generally a good predictor of future behavior, some ex-offenders can be extremely valuable employees. People often learn lessons the hard way.

Third, appeal to your employees' motivation so they are less likely to want to steal in the first place. People who steal are often angry at the way they have been treated.

Finally, directly address your managers' supervisory skills, since they're any company's first line of defense. Focus on skills in coaching and performance assessment to start.

If you're wondering what my advice to Ron and Carl was, I'll tell you. I had none. I simply asked, do you really want to work for a company that doesn't trust you?

@DrJanice: If you are in a job where you have no support, no team, no vision or mission, please don't blame yourself for job failure.

I've always thought of myself as a pretty good person, but I've been on some pretty bad teams. What went wrong? Google had no answers, but eventually I broke the code.

When Good People Make Bad Teams

I googled 'teamwork' one day and got a zillion pages of useless garbage. Most of them seemed to be talking about teams of oxen: Just work together and move in the same direction, be nice to each other and all will be fine. Shades of **Brave New World**! Is this what we want for our businesses in the twenty-first century? Is this the way to meet our global competition?

How teams go wrong

Okay, I didn't learn much new from Google that day, but I did get some of my hypotheses reconfirmed. Teams like those can work well together if all you expect from them is that they do exactly what you tell them to do, when you want it, and you check up on every little thing they do. Pay them well, give them soothing background music and keep their work hours short, fire the rebels, and you can have what you want pretty easily. If this actually appeals to you, you probably thought "The Stepford Wives" was utopian. But if the concept makes you just a little uncomfortable, think about this: You would be paying people to pretend to be computerized robots, and you can do that cheaper with the real thing.

The people who can make your business grow profitably have one quality in common: creativity. The caveat is they aren't all creative in the same way. Try googling creativity and you won't do much better than I did with teamwork. There are a lot of creativity tests on the web, each complete with right answers.

The problem? Creativity involves discovering the answer that hasn't been thought of yet.

So if what you are trying to do is put together a team that will operate as a creativity production unit, and you've started out with good people, here are five sure ways to turn them into a bad team.

1. Make sure they aren't allowed to implement any decisions. Remind them of this on a regular basis. The better you are at micromanagement the easier this will be. You'll know you are successful when not only can meeting attendance barely be achieved by making it mandatory but also the team members actively avoid each other – even at the water cooler.

2. Avoid, at all costs, any Role diversity on the team. Role diversity differs from the usual thing people think of when they hear the word diversity. It means that different team members have different styles of thinking and manners of approaching a problem's solution.

3. Create a culture of secrecy and mistrust, but above all, prevent any form of faith from becoming part of it. A truly dysfunctional organization is quite powerful, demanding almost cult-like loyalty. It forces people into dysfunctional Roles for survival, and these tend to reproduce themselves prolifically, thus ensuring that good people will continue to form bad teams no matter what.

4. Remember that knowledge is power. Keep your staff in the dark unless they have a need to know. This demonstrates clearly that you don't trust them.

5. Show them the same respect you would show to any other interchangeable part. They can easily be replaced.

Managing your team to success

We will assume that if you have read this far that you are either the leader of a team or someone who wishes that their team leader, whether line supervisor or CEO, were reading along with you. You certainly have permission to share this. In fact, feel free to blame it on me by telling your team leader that Dr. Janice asked you to pass it on to him or her. (If it gets you into trouble, I will be happy to write a note for you. As Fran Lebowitz said, "It's not whether you win or lose, it's how you lay the blame." This is the basic principle of failing organizations.)

If you are leading a team, you are, *de facto*, what we call its Founder. While this may or may not be your primary or even secondary Role preference, you are there because someone else believes in your ability (or didn't see any alternative, which in the end doesn't really matter if you are in the position.) If you started your own business, no matter how small it is, you are definitely the Founder and probably have at least some liking for it. (If you don't, you are probably doing something you know how to do, but would really prefer to be doing it for someone else's organization.)

If the objective is to create a coherent human infrastructure, I ask only three things of people:

- that they work with their team toward mutual trust that each will do their part

- that they show respect for each other in the way that person best experiences it, and

- that they actively demonstrate faith that the overall goal is worthwhile.

Part of working together as a team is sharing what strengths you have and giving them freely to your teammates, rather than worrying about the strengths you don't have.

This is why having a diverse set of Roles represented on your team will give you the best chance of having someone who loves doing those things you hate doing and aren't very good at.

On a team with all Founders (or all any other Role) teamwork and creativity are lost in a tangle of multiple versions of vision and mission. In football, no matter how spectacular the wide receiver may be, you can't have a winning football team when everyone is best suited to be a wide receiver.

Whatever your own style of team behavior (what we call your primary Role preference) may be, meshing solidly with the Role that leads the team will strengthen the value you bring to the team, yourself and your organization because you will add your own unique strengths. Here are some suggestions for strengthening your leadership skills:

- Write your Vision paper. This is a formal statement that shows what you are going to accomplish and how it is an inevitable advance in your field. If your team doesn't do it, someone else will.

- Even if all you can manage at first is a sentence or two, it will help you light a beacon to attract, excite, and motivate your team. It doesn't matter if it is big or small, entrepreneurial or personal, wide-ranging or narrowly focused. Just start. (If you've already done this make sure you update it periodically, and don't forget to pass it down through your team.)

- Practice inspiring people. This is easy if you have small children around, because it is very easy to inspire a child. (Unfortunately the reverse is also true. They are un-inspired by the same things that un-inspire adults: sarcasm, unfair treatment, scapegoating, etc.) If you don't have a team of your own around to inspire, become a mentor to someone. You will get more out of the relationship than you give, so be sure to give a lot. If you can give without thinking about what you are getting, that is even better.

- If you are lucky enough to be at the point where you have a team to help you achieve your Vision, be sure to feed them. This can mean providing snacks for a meeting but more often it is providing food for mind and soul. Set out your platter of wisdom, ideas, plans, dreams, and information, and encourage them to taste a bit of everything. Figure out how to give them 'doggie bags' to take with them, because this is a self-regenerating platter that grows as you give.

- Create an enjoyable workspace for your team. It can be as simple as having some foam rubber balls to toss around for fun or as elaborate as installing a pool table in the lunch area, but do it with the heart of a host.

- Praise the members of your team for their work, on a frequent basis. You can never give enough positive feedback to those who help your Vision come true. This is above and beyond the other kinds of rewards that people like – such as cold hard cash and those gifts that really are the same. Just forget the motivational items that will seem trivial, match your 'thanks for a great job' to the individual (understanding their Role will guide you), and wherever possible make the praise and thanks public and with something to take home. (Remember Mom hanging your 'A' papers and prize artwork on the refrigerator? How about taking a picture and posting it someplace?)

- Tell the story of your team to people, both inside and outside your organization, who can help them. Storytelling is the art and responsibility of the Founder.

Even if you do all of this, you will still have to put together a team with people who think in diverse ways. The more you have people you are comfortable with and who think just like you do, the more you will see exactly what you have always seen, and the more you will do what you have always done. Even if you have been successful in the past, the market is in a constant state of change. The highway to sustainable success is littered with the failures of those who drove on, believing so much that the path never curves that they didn't recognize any until after they drove off the road.

@DrJanice: Trust, empowerment, encouragement, self-management... that's the recipe for getting the best out of people.

Someone asked me to give a brief talk on this subject. While most people, they say, can't absorb more than three ideas, I hated to waste the other 21 I came up with, so they ended up in this blog.

Two Dozen Ideas to Help You Develop & Keep Your Best Employees

1. Know your employees – talk to them and, even more important, listen to them. They won't all respond to the same ideas.

2. Encourage collaboration between employees and departments. It's a good way to make one and one add up to more than two.

3. Promote the benefits of professional and personal development to everyone in your organization. Set a good example by talking about what you learn every day.

4. If you are running a family business, minimize the traditional barriers that non-family employees face in hiring and promotion decisions.

5. Be a good corporate neighbor and seek a positive reputation in your community.

6. Acknowledge the importance of your employees' home lives and help them integrate work and home priorities. Be known as a family-friendly company, and please consider that not all families are the traditional husband, wife, and 2.4 children.

7. Offer a wide range of benefits, both employer and employee paid, that meet employees' expressed needs.

8. Offer flexible work time arrangements if at all possible – job sharing, part time and temporary employment will expand your pool of possible hires.

9. Reward your senior managers for living your vision, setting a good example, and communicating openly, frequently, and well to the people they manage.

10. Educate yourself and your managers about the high cost of turnover and reward them for their successes in minimizing it.

11. Publicly recognize people when they do a good job. A smile, a thank you, and a handshake from you in the presence of an employee's peers will be a strong motivator for most people (other than the very, very shy).

12. Create a physical setting conducive to productivity. Seek employee input on this!

13. Remind your workers – and yourself – about the importance of your customers and treat your employees at least as well as your customers.

14. Help your employees prepare for career opportunities within your company. Offer training, coaching, mentoring – and your personal commitment.

15. Conduct exit interviews with all terminating employees and value their input.

16. If you talk the talk, be prepared to walk the walk.

17. Don't badmouth the competition in front of employees – you might make them curious.

18. Being open about succession planning helps people feel secure that the company will go on.

19. Keep rumors under control by sharing information, positive and negative, before they start.

20. Don't make promises you can't – or won't – keep.

21. Don't rationalize not giving salary raises by saying the company's in trouble and then drive to work in a new luxury car.

22. Treat your older workers with respect. Tell them you value their experience and ask them to share it by mentoring a new employee.

23. Treat your younger workers well by challenging them to develop initiative – and when they do, try not to micromanage them.

24. When all else fails, break the tension and bring people together with a shared laugh.

@DrJanice: Great followers are great leaders, and vice versa. #Leadership is a team sport. #Teamability

Part 3: Leadership is a Team Sport

I truly believe that leadership is a team sport. Some people say that's because it's the only team sport I've ever played. The truth is, even though my nickname is DrJ like the great Dr. Julius Erving, there's not much resemblance. I'm 5'2", can't lift weights or run fast, and you won't find a giant mural painting of me anywhere in Philadelphia…but I do have a mean hook shot (in the paint).

The thing about playing leadership as a team sport is that it requires <u>teaming</u>. And that's what I've spent a good part of my life doing, while developing theory, method, and, finally, new technology that measures how people will perform on a team. It's called Teamability®, and it's pretty revolutionary if I do say so myself. (You already know I am a sixties person. We tend to lean in that direction.)

Many of the chapters that follow call for an understanding of the basic principles of Teamability, so let's start with those.

Teamability is not derived from personality or IQ testing, from EQ, strengths, or engagement surveys, or from any other familiar tools or methods. It identifies some very useful – and practical – metrics of teaming. They include:

- ***Role***: *a person's affinity for specific modes of service to the needs of a team*

- ***Coherence***: *expressed as positive, flexible, constructive teaming behaviors*

- ***Teaming Characteristics***: *individual styles of responding and relating to others, subject to situational context*

- **Role-respect**: *the unique manner in which people of different Roles experience appreciation and respect*

- **Role-pairing**: *known, replicable synergies between specific Roles*

- **Role-fit**: *an appropriate match between a person's Role and their assigned set of job responsibilities*

- **Team-fit:** *structuring a team to include the Roles that are best-fit to the team's mission*

This new way to know about teaming behavior was initially referred to as Role-Based Assessment (RBA). Formal research and field validation studies were conducted over a period of ten years, through three separate iterations of design and development. With each iteration, successively higher levels of correlation were found between the content of the reports and the observed workplace behavior of participants. As it became increasingly clear that a person's Role was a crucial factor in the quality of team interaction, teaming technology and the Role-based approach to understanding team performance gradually merged into the single, simple concept of Teamability.

A most important aspect of Teamability is that it produces measurable business value. One compelling example is the SuperNova® prize for emerging technology, awarded by Constellation Research to Preferred Sands a $1 billion firm based near Philadelphia, PA. There, the use of Teamability resulted in rapid resolution of team performance problems, and extraordinary gains in quality-of-hire.

Business benefits from the use of Teamability have been further verified by the experiences and testimonials of managers, executives, and business owners in various market segments and functional areas of business, from startups to giant corporations and institutions.

Teamability®:

- *the ability to connect with others to form a productive team*

- *the ability to communicate in a coherent manner with the intent to enhance team spirit*

- *the most prominent characteristic of a team member*

- *a set of predictive metrics encompassing one's Role, Coherence, and Teaming Characteristics as defined by TGI's Role-based approach to the understanding of team synergy*

- *a portfolio of new methods for selecting, developing, managing, and motivating both individuals and teams*

@DrJanice: Stress will derail even the best team. Leaders reduce it well.

My first job felt like I was wearing my mother's dress: too big for me to be comfortable in. My second felt like I was wearing my baby daughter's jeans: way too small! It was then that I started thinking about how 'fit' works in a business environment.

Predicting Business Leadership Excellence

It's perhaps the worst kept secret in the business world that what you know is worth only about 25% as a predictor of whether or not you will succeed. The rest is based on fit – how you fit with your boss, your team, your customers and your organization's culture.

If you've ever been fired because the boss just didn't appreciate you, or you've left a job because of a boss you just could not stand to work for one more moment, or because you knew there were options that would be so much more fulfilling, you know what I'm talking about. Take me, for instance. I didn't get into a job that actually fit me until after I'd worked my way through many wrong turns, numerous missteps, and even some outright failures. While at the time I would not have chosen to experience so many quandaries and predicaments, and while they certainly didn't always feel like positive experiences, in the end I realize that – collectively – they had a deep and beneficial effect. They've made me unusually realistic, empathetic, and flexible. These three characteristics do not appear in my current job description, but may nevertheless be some of the most important qualifiers I bring to the office.

Looking back, I realize that none of those jobs were dreadful, distasteful, or stultifying in and of themselves, any more than I was inadequate, overeducated, under-experienced, or way too ambitious for my own good. We (the jobs and I) were not the right fit for each other, and that was no one's fault. But the misfits did prevent me — and the organizations where I held them — from being excellent. (In case you are curious, I finally did get a job that I was right for. I'm CEO of a company that has created an innovative technology of teaming.)

So what does all this mean for business leadership? In today's economy, the need to do more with less impacts everything you do to bring value to your company. It can mean the difference between recognition as a value-creating member of the management team and being marginalized as pure overhead. To cover the likelihood that the economic recovery will continue its slow ascent, you need both a short-term strategy, and a long-term vision that will prepare your organization to respond proactively to a shift in either the pace, or the direction, of economic growth. And if you want to get some 'insurance' for yourself and your people, you'll need something else: metrics that prove the efficiency and effectiveness of your team!

The first challenge in a downturn is to confront this simple truth: people who were the right people during good times may not be right during bad times. Resolving this conundrum is a way to add real value. Start with some quantifiable data. Has there been an increase in people problems? Are you hearing from more managers that their teams seem distracted or demoralized? Are your standard productivity measures off, your accident counts rising, your undesired terminations soaring?

Next, do some qualitative research. Do your people actually behave in the workplace as expected? Are they meeting their goals? Are they doing this in a way that helps other people achieve their goals too? Do you see measurable effects of synergy between people, or are they cancelling out each other's efforts?

Finally, can you link their behavior to the organization's bottom line? If they are the right fit in all (or most) ways — with their boss, their team mates, the desired organizational culture — then they are likely to be more globally productive, and you should be able to track this in the output of the work teams, no matter how that output is measured.

Clearly, a metric that correlates with positive team interaction would be of great value, and in fact it is now possible to obtain a simple predictor of overall effectiveness. It indicates that the individual is capable of rising to the occasion, dealing with the stresses of having to do more with less, accepting ambiguities and the inability to predict what the business environment will be like tomorrow, and forging ahead nonetheless. That predictor is called Coherence. It's a measure of how much flexibility and willingness there is to flow with the rest of the team, and conversely, how much stress it takes to send someone off-kilter, which is usually experienced as fear or anxiety. Effective, productive coherent people who team well are far more likely to produce measurable positive synergies, even in a less-than-optimal business environment.

So, what about people who are less coherent? Under stress, some become rigid and overbearing to the point that they interfere with the flow of work. Others will avoid problems they don't want to face, or misdirect attention by blaming others. If the pressure gets really intense, hostile (even violent) behavior may arise. At the other extreme, think of people who fall apart when the going gets tough. They are diffuse. They may be friendly and likable, and they often have a knack for surviving—despite their lack of commitment to making consistent and meaningful contributions to the team. You may not even realize that that you've been doing some of their work, in addition to your own.

Let's not jump to conclusions here. Less coherent people can still do excellent work, and can deliver value on teams. However, when the going gets rough, or when significant change comes down the pike and you need to assemble a high-impact survival team, elevated Coherence becomes essential. Under such circumstances, an informed leader will find less stressful assignments for the others.

In addition to identifying and properly aligning coherent people, you can also encourage and develop the overall level of Coherence on a team in other ways. Here are a few:

- First, get a baseline measurement of the overall Coherence of your organization. Start with your own team and work your way through the others. (A Teamability pilot project will be a good start in establishing this metric.)

- Learn about Teamability Roles and how each different Role is best suited to certain kinds of job responsibilities. Then spend some time aligning the responsibilities of people on your team with their own specific Role. This is called Role-fit, and when done right, it will invariably reduce stress and increase positive team synergy.

- Examine each team for diversity of Roles. Too much homogeneity can inhibit – or even damage – team performance. You may need to reconsider recruiting and other talent management policies, which may actually be ruling out some of the very Roles you need most.

- When you have people with a burning desire for better Role-fit with their job, find a way to make it happen—with minimal risk to the organization but with maximum stretch room and support. If you don't have a formal mentoring program, start one.

- Get all your managers on board by starting with them. Show them the metrics, and the predictors. Then help them engage with each other to build a culture that will support the excellence you are seeking.

- Finally, to establish the relationship between your actions and the positive team outcomes, don't forget to validate with appropriate metrics. You'll be adding value to your organization as well as proving that you too are excellent!

@DrJanice: #BigData can only help if it is relevant. I prefer #BigWisdom.

There are questions you can freely ask anyone. Just check anything ever written about networking. Then there are the ones that require you to tread more carefully when you ask them. Those are the questions that have always interested me the most.

I May Not Have All the Answers, But I Have Some Good Questions

Maybe it's my line of work, but people are always expecting me to have the answers. (If they got a Teamability report from my company, it will contain a lot of answers. But from me? – sorry, I didn't replace my crystal ball when it broke, and since we started using Keurig coffee pods at the office, there aren't enough tea leaves around here for a decent reading.)

So instead of feeling useless, answer-wise, I thought I'd give you a look at some of my favorite questions.

Warning: The Surgeon General has determined that you may safely ask these questions of yourself. However, asking them of other people, without an explicit request for help, can be dangerous to your health. (And that warning goes double if you happen to be married to the respondent!)

"What does that mean?"

It's always a good idea to start by defining your terms and concepts. Language is rich, but if you don't establish a common frame of reference, you will get noise and distortion in the communication channels. When that happens, it is easy to end up thinking that you understand, even when you are missing the point – totally. This guarantees that many, if not most, of the answers anyone comes up with during the course of the discussion will not be helpful ones.

"How do you know?"

We have browsers. We have Google. We have expert communities. With all the stuff that the giant collective 'they' opines about on practically any topic, it's amazing how much trouble we still get ourselves into. That's because we are sometimes entirely too dependent on what 'they' know. (If you don't believe me, visit and snoop around Snopes.com.) A lot of the stuff we 'know' because 'they' said it, just isn't so. Sometimes asking the 'How' question snaps us back into reality.

"So what?"

People often want advice on how to change things that they have no power to change – or even to connect with. I don't want to offend any change management professionals here. Changing big organizational processes is a tough challenge. But sometimes change doesn't warrant all the hue and cry that goes up when people first hear about it. So when someone is complaining, and there's really not much substance to it, you can hit them with 'So what?' It's especially effective when used sparingly – and sincerely. You'll sound practical – and sympathetic – at the same time, and you won't actually have to get too deeply involved with sound and fury that signifies nothing.

"Why?"

I love this question the most because kids ask it all the time. And it has the simplest answer (ask any tired parent): "Because." The key with this question, for adults as much as for any kid, is that sometimes you need to keep asking it until you get an answer that satisfies you. And on the flip side – you can just keep giving this answer until the person expecting a different, better one, goes off to search elsewhere.

Lastly, a favorite question, and of a much higher order: Hamlet's "To be or not to be?"

Only one good answer. Be.

Be-cause when you are be-ing, good questions (and good answers) sorta come naturally.

@DrJanice: Leadership is a team sport. I think we proved that being a jerk at the top doesn't cut it any more.

You might want to reread this after you've read the Afterword. It will explain a lot about what really does seem inexplicable.

Random Acts of Naughtiness

December hadn't even started yet when Forbes named the top CEO screw-ups of 2010.

The undisputed champion is **Tony Hayward** – a man who, upon his appointment as CEO of British Petroleum, promised a "laser-like focus on safety and reliability." In addition to having an oral fixation on his own foot, his laser apparently missed safety entirely and instead scored a direct hit on the Deepwater Horizon during drilling operations.

Joining this ex-CEO in the 'bonehead hall of fame' are, in no particular order:

Michael Lyon, ex-CEO of his family's huge real estate company, was arraigned on charges of secretly making home videos of his 'liaisons dangereuses' with paid escorts. The company's new CEO is now busy trying to recruit agents away from other companies. I wonder if they also videotape their interview process?

Jon Latorella, ex-CEO of Locateplus, was indicted on charges of securities fraud, filing false statements to the company's auditor and the SEC, aggravated theft, and a few, even juicier, charges. Adding just a touch of irony, Locateplus describes itself as the industry leader in providing online investigative solutions to law enforcement. Lesson learned: Don't cheat where you eat!

Carly Fiorina, former Hewlett-Packard CEO. While en route to her failed bid to become a U.S. Senator, Ms. Fiorina criticized

Barbara Boxer's hair instead of her policies. Now, now, ladies… There are too few of us in leadership already. Let's not allow healthy competition to devolve into cat-fighting!

Linda McMahon, who also flopped as a U.S. Senate seat seeker, did herself no favors by admitting that she 'had no idea' whether or not World Wrestling Entertainment, her previous CEO gig, had paid its employees at least the state-mandated minimum wage. Listen up, Linda…just a little girlfriend advice. When you apply for a job, it's a good idea to do a little research.

Timothy Huff, former GlobeTel CEO, was sentenced to 50 months in prison after pleading guilty to charges of conspiring with his CFO to create fake revenue, report it, and then fabricate invoices and documents to back up the non-existent numbers. And, get ready…Tim isn't the first C-level GlobeTel Executive to be indicted. He follows in the footsteps of Thomas Jimenez, convicted of tax fraud for failing to report over $2.7 million in GlobeTel stock grants (to himself and others) as income. Who says corporate culture isn't important?

And the Forbes list of 'winner' CEOs goes on and on: I.O. Hawkins of Petro America; Gary Holden of Enmax; Lei Jin of GeneScience Pharma, and the incomparable cheesiness of HP's Mark Hurd. But in case all this bad behavior is just too much for you, think back to Bernie Madoff, who cooked up $50 billion worth of fraud, betrayal, and financial ruination.

So is bad behavior something we should just come to expect from CEOs? I hope not. I mean, I'm a CEO, and even if I had the inclination to do bad things (which I don't), I would never risk subjecting my family, my investors, or my team to such disappointment and shame.

These CEO's were called Leaders, but their behaviors had nothing to do with leadership; just self-interest and an utter lack of 'team' sensibility.

Leadership is a team sport. If you aren't a good team player, you can't be a good leader.

@DrJanice: Stop hiring managers who can't manage people they can't stand over. #leadership #fail

One day I was waiting to meet with someone who reports directly to a CEO. In fact, they were in the CEO's office interviewing a potential senior executive. For some reason, his assistant seated me outside the CEO's office where I inadvertently overheard the interview. Rather, where I overheard the CEO pontificate on what I surmised was the interviewee's area of expertise. It went on for 35 minutes. I never even heard a word uttered by the interviewee. I later learned that she was hired. The CEO, who shall remain nameless, inspired this blog.

Five Thoughts on Interviewing, Plus One Just for Leaders

1. **Shut up and listen**: Every moment you speak is a moment your interviewee is silent. Unless you are interviewing someone who will be working for you as a mime, you aren't learning anything while you're talking.

2. **Ask SPIN questions**: Help your interviewee learn more about the position and company—while you're learning more about them—by asking them value-centric questions. Try using what sales guru Neil Rackham, author of *SPIN Selling* and many other books on business communication, calls 'Implication' and 'Need-payoff' questions. For example, "What if you got this position and could do anything within reason to make it a success?" Or, "Here's a recurring problem (describe it); how many kinds of adverse impact on our business can you identify?" This gives candidates an opportunity to dig in and actually sell themselves on the job opportunity, while giving you a view into their thinking and problem solving processes.

3. **Stick to a plan:** Remember that an interview is a form of assessment. If every interview follows a different path,

there can be no accurate or reasonable comparison between candidates. Not only do you need to ask the same questions of each interviewee, you need to interpret their answers in the same way. Furthermore, if you don't isolate the key message points and stay focused on them, it is all the more likely that the candidate's physical characteristics, gender, race, nationality, style of dress, etc. will creep into the assessment – and before you know it you will be adrift in unconscious biases that can lead to future trouble.

4. **Pick a team player**: Use the assessment that was designed to measure teaming characteristics. Hiring has always been focused primarily on the attributes of the individual candidates. Ironically, how well they will perform on the team doesn't come to the fore until after the hire, and isn't recognized as a failing until after the bad hire has done plenty of damage. You can't really ask people how they team and expect a reliable answer, so you need a way to predict how they will behave.

5. **Take the high road**: Even when you're having a tough day, remember that you are making decisions of critical importance to your organization. You have direct influence on building and maintaining a human infrastructure that will determine the success or failure of your entire organization. Take a deep breath, ask for a second opinion if you're unsure, and always keep learning.

And for Leaders:

Remember, you are picking someone who will be teaming with you. Do you know what your own teaming characteristics are? Don't fight them: they've gotten you this far so don't mess with success. Just make sure the person you're bringing in will bring three things to the job: a Role complementary to yours, Coherence at the level you require, and the kind of Teaming Characteristics that spell success on your team. When you're building your human infrastructure, you may as well build from your own specs!

@DrJanice: Stop doing annual reviews and just talk to your people. Try thanking them. #leadership

When I was young, I had all the answers. It took me a long time to learn that answers are the easy part.

The Questions of Leadership

When you're on the first rung of the leadership ladder, you get your first experience in evaluating people. My first experience involved some pretty useless forms that someone got out of a book. They weren't bad or evil. They just bore no resemblance to what was truly important to the organization.

I've never liked the idea of New Year's resolutions, but that year I made one. It was to think more about the right questions to ask my team than the right answers to give them. These might not be the ones you would ask, but they are the ones I thought of for my own team so maybe they will be useful for yours.

1. Do you understand the Founder's Vision?

2. Is the Vision personally relevant to you?

3. Do you understand what the plan is to reach the Vision?

4. Do you know what your part of the action is in the organization's quest for the Vision?

5. Do you have the tools you need to do your part?

6. Are people generally approachable when you need help?

7. Do you have one or two particular people with whom you do *great* work?

8. Does it feel like there is enough to go around at the company or do you feel like you have to share paper clips and ration coffee?

9. Do you get frequent updates on where the organization is on its quest?

10. Do you feel energized by your work?

11. Do you find yourself thinking about things you could do that haven't been assigned to you or aren't in your job description or on your task list?

12. Do you feel connected to others at work – both teammates and customers?

13. Do you feel you have a mission that is like a spiritual one?

14. Does it seem natural to be doing what you are doing?

15. Are you given enough responsibility at work?

16. Are you given enough respect at work?

17. Are you given enough rewards at work?

18. Are you given the kind of rewards you like?

19. Are you given the kind of feedback you like?

20. Are you given enough feedback at the right time?

In case you're wondering, I didn't hand this out as an assignment. I thought of it as more of a gift. Not the questions as a gift to them. Their answers as a gift to me.

@DrJanice: You set the biz model, then the culture. Then you get to be the spokesmodel. I love my job. #CEO

When some people find out I've been measuring leaders for a long time, they ask me for a quick and easy way to know who's right for leadership. (They never actually ask me for accurate predictions; only reassurance that they're ok.) So I devised this test, just for them.

Winning Leadership: The Real Score

People who think they can be everything to everyone fascinate me, especially when it comes to leadership. This is a quiz designed to frustrate them because you have to choose only one from each pair. Even worse, I'm going to ask you to honestly consider how you actually behave, not what you think you would do or what you would like to do. Are you game?

Choose A or B:

A: My job is to inspire my team, so I share my vision with them and seek their input.
OR
B: My job is to motivate my team, so I set goals and reward them for a job well done.

Choose A or B:

A: I spend some time most days focusing on where I want to go.
OR
B: I spend some time most days focusing on achieving the desired outcomes.

Choose A or B:

A: I know where I'm going and I trust my team to follow.
OR
B: I frequently check in and herd my team so they don't get lost as they work toward the goals.

Choose A or B:

A: I explain what I want to my team as they seem to need it.
OR
B: I have documented very clear rules and I expect my team to follow them.

Choose A or B:

A: I give my team wide berth to do their jobs in the way that makes sense to them.
OR
B: I am careful to set reasonable limits on how far people are allowed to deviate from my plans.

Choose A or B:

A: I thank my team for being there.
OR
B: I praise my team for doing things well.

Add up your As and your Bs and don't be too concerned which you had more of. You are who you are: if you have more As, most people would say you're more of a leader. If you have more Bs, they'd say you're more of a manager. One isn't better than the other; they're just different.

But that's not the real score.

To get your real score, answer these two questions:

1. In how many instances was it very difficult for you to choose only one option? (The more difficult, the more likely you actually are capable of doing both, which is, after all, what needs to get done if you're going to have anything to lead.)

2. In how many instances did you think of someone else on your team who prefers the opposite of your choice? (The greater the number, the more likely you focus on the team rather than yourself.)

The real score is that leadership happens when you're not thinking about it. It happens when you focus so much on supporting other people that they can't think of you as anything other than their leader.

@DrJanice: If your job isn't satisfying in all ways, why would you want to stay with it?

As I've already said, I was not raised to be an entrepreneur, and maybe I would never have become one but for the pull that inventing Teamability has had on me for so long. But maybe, if I were an unemployed executive like so many of my friends. I would now be at my wits' end, ready to try anything.

A Modest Proposal for the Unemployment Problem

I hope we can agree on one thing: unemployment isn't good for anyone. It's not just that idle hands are the devil's workshop, but that long-term unemployment scares all of us, even the currently employed. And fear erodes our engagement, reduces our productivity, and stifles our innovative spirit.

Entrepreneurs play a major part in driving innovation and a growing economy. According to a study by the Kauffman Foundation (the world's largest non-profit foundation dedicated to the support of entrepreneurship), entrepreneurs and their startup teams are, and have been, the ONLY source of net new jobs in almost every year since 1977! (The chart below reveals how startups have consistently created new jobs, compared to existing organizations.)

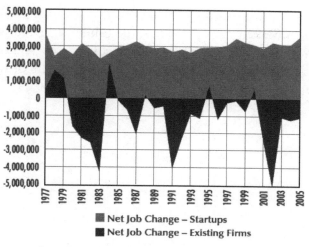

Net Job Change – Startups
Net Job Change – Existing Firms

Source: Business Dynamics Statistics, Tim Kane

Unfortunately, the balance between jobs disappearing and jobs being created is only part of the problem. Are you trapped in a job that you really don't fit, or worse, trapped in one that makes you miserable? Without a vibrant job market, getting stuck like this has become a serious problem.

My Advice

If you're entrepreneurial, give your ideas a chance. Organizations that help start-ups are popping up everywhere. Find a way to bootstrap your idea with the help of anyone who's willing to help you – especially if they approach the challenge from directions you haven't thought of yet.

If you're in HR, please recognize that resumes are losing their relevance, and work requirements are being transformed. Look to the emerging field of Talent Science for alternatives. For most jobs, understanding how a person teams with others is at least as important as current and past employment. (Have you noticed that 401k documents say something like "past performance is not a guarantee of future performance?" That's because it isn't.)

If you're looking, resist the temptation to apply for jobs you know you are likely to hate. Take some time to learn how you really want to contribute to the mission of an organization. Then articulate the key points, and communicate them widely. Social media – it's not just for socializing any more.

@DrJanice: Employer loyalty drives employee loyalty. Not the other way round. #leadership

It's almost counterintuitive: the more powerful someone is, the more likely they are to trust others, not mistrust them. Part of the reason has to do with the source of their power. They recognize that they have it, but also that they aren't the ultimate source of it. They've got humility and they're not afraid to show it.

Humility Breeds Trust

Since so many CEO failures are caused by failure to put the right people in the right job, and the related failure to fix people problems before they blow up, the big question is, why do such smart people make such bad decisions?

One reason: approaching the problem while believing that you already know the solution. Starting with a full mind leaves no room for new perceptions. Performance is highly linked to how much trust is present in the DNA of the culture. And it often seems we know more about how to destroy that trust than we know about building it.

Most people's default setting is to trust others and to expect to be trusted. They assume that everyone is headed in the same direction, toward the achievement of the vision. Then they crash into someone who neither respects nor returns that trust. This is their first experience of disenchantment.

Sometimes it's the rigid, Machiavellian boss who promises you'll get to try your wings on an exciting project and then clips them mid-air. Sometimes it's the co-worker who has little original thinking but is happy to take credit for your work.

If you want to lead a trust-based organization, you should start by focusing on bottom-line results. If you believe the hype about leaders, you'll think that all it takes is a lot of charisma and a great story. That helps. But neither vision nor execution alone will deliver bottom-line results – they require vision plus planning plus execution plus follow through.

You can't do all that yourself. No one can focus on all of these at the same time and accomplish them at a high level. Teams can achieve what an individual cannot, but only if there is diversity of style and focus, and a leader who realizes that no one person can be everything. Humility will keep you from flying into the sun, unlike poor Icarus who was gifted with many qualities of leadership – save the humility that would have allowed him to listen to others who warned him that things were going to heat up far beyond his control.

Here are some suggestions for building your trust-based organization:

- You don't have to be a member of a 12-step program to take a fearless inventory. Does your default setting indicate arrogance or humility? Do you really know how you affect those who work with and for you?

- Remember to balance the needs of the organization with the needs of the people. You won't know what those needs are unless you know people as individuals and understand what motivates them. A good measure of your humility will be your lack of surprise when you realize that what motivates you most is not necessarily what motivates them most.

- Understand that there is great value in the diversity of other people's styles and Roles. People who don't think the way you do are tremendously valuable to you in solving problems and coming up with innovative ideas. Listen carefully to all of them, and understand each point of view and carefully consider it even if, at first, you don't agree with the premise. If you turn it down, do so with respect and gratitude for their act of trusting you with it.

- Earn the best team you can get. Engage them in your process – vision, execution, evaluation – and make it a living process. Set team goals that are challenging but attainable and lavishly reward the entire team for achieving them. Rewards can be non-financial and just as effective as long as they are oriented to what motivates each individual.

Remember your origins. You were not born to lead at birth. Someone trusted you. Now it is your turn to trust and to be trustworthy. The further you get from your origins, the further from Earth you will fly until, like Icarus, you are left with no supports, and your fall is inevitable.

@DrJanice: You can have a better teaming relationship with someone across the world than across the hall. Really. #Teamability

This blog was inspired not only by this experience in flight, but also by a brief phone interchange with Raj Munusamy, VP of Global Marketing at Siemens Enterprise, whom I hereby acknowledge as a 'who' of great personal value to me.

Is There a Future of Teamwork?

Let me start with the assertion that I am not a Luddite. Far from rejecting new technology, I was an early adopter of just about any form of it that I came across, and I have never regretted it. Not even for some of the technologies that bombed. But recently, I became painfully aware that willy-nilly technology adoption may be a root cause of problems that many companies are having with their teams, especially their distance (or virtual) teams.

The convenience, and ever-presence, of technology may be turning us into nation of non-connectors. And if you don't connect with other people, how can you team successfully?

Let me explain…

I'm writing this while sitting in first class on a plane, going to speak at a conference. I've done this many times during the course of my long career, and not so long ago, business people would signify their status through business-appropriate garb and appropriate accessories. Secure in their status, those same business people would typically spend social moments during the flight – takeoff, meals, landing – chatting with seatmates. In fact, travelers often made the decision to fly first or business class based on the potential quality of networking connections, in addition to the extra comforts. But no more. TSA regulations discourage the wearing of metallic objects, and the urge to travel light has greatly increased the appeal of casual dress.

So, on this flight, where there are twelve seats in the forward cabin, there is no discourse at all, excepting between three men who clearly are traveling together; perhaps old college buddies as I gather from a few tidbits of their banter. Among the rest, I don't even see an acknowledgment that there is a person sitting in the adjacent seat – much less a conversation.

Typically, when in groups, people will seek and share commonalities that act as social lubricants, and what easier commonality is there than the knowledge we are all traveling to the same destination? Doesn't anyone here think there may be value to be found? Has all curiosity been drained out of us?

Going back in time, I remember one flight in particular. I took my seat next to a gentleman dressed in a fine suit and tie. We acknowledged each other's presence and shared pleasantries during boarding, and then he politely mentioned he was on his way to mentor a company and had to review a number of documents to prepare. I smiled and mentioned that I, too, had work to do. Two laptops were booted, two seatmates did productive work, and then lunch was served. The laptops were closed and the conversation began again. I found that he had considerable experience running companies similar to mine. We became 'who's to each other. Not just a 'what' occupying adjacent space. And so we shared anecdotes and enjoyed each other's company. Lunch ended, and we returned to our work. For me, at least, there was value gained, and it showed itself in the plan I had been working on. I hope I gave my fellow traveler at least a small measure of similar value.

Today, all I see are solitary heads with wires trailing from earlobes. It isn't that I don't like music. (For proof, ask Pandora, iTunes, Spotify, 8tracks, or I could post a snapshot of the CDs still rattling around the back seat of my car.) What troubles me is that, from all appearances, isolation is becoming the new normal.

If every child has a smartphone and earbuds, and every phone plan or cable station has entertainment that you get to choose for yourself at all times (no more taking turns choosing what to watch or hear!), how does that impact a person's development as a team player?

It is hard enough to form a functional team in the midst of all the normal distractions and frustrations of the world. But people have learned, through practice from childhood on, to filter out these distractions. We actually start at the moment of birth, learning to team with our mother to retrieve the food and comforts formerly provided automatically *in utero*. We continue learning to team as we navigate the intricacies of relating to one other, then two others, and then several people, in a consistent manner. For example, we learn that telling mom one thing and dad another is unlikely to work well for us. The noise and interference that we encounter pose enormous challenges, but we discover that the prize is worth the effort. And with practice we become team-able.

What will happen when we no longer have the opportunity to practice?

@DrJanice: Sometimes learning sneaks in while you thought you were just being social. #Teamability

Not a Born Leader? So What!

I was not born a leader.

When I was born (and this was a very long time ago), there were serious defects in my leadership blueprint. First, I had two X chromosomes at a time when one Y was needed in order to be a leader. Actually, nobody knew what a chromosome was back then, so 42 Extra Long was the preferred measure, and I didn't reach my full 5'2" until I was 25.

Although I had no choice in the matter, I also ended up with two loving parents, neither of which was entrepreneur or executive. It would seem hopeless.

Now, in 2013, diversity is desirable. My dear friends in executive search tell me that they are under the gun to produce diversity slates for the high level positions they are engaged to fill. A diversity slate, one told me with his typically charming sense of irony is one that includes at least one woman and one non-white. When pressed to explain, he went on to say that this configuration positioned the first runner up to be the feel-good candidate while there actually would be no danger of hiring a person other than someone who looked like the rest of the executive team.

I think we're looking at the wrong kind of diversity.

What if, instead, we looked at people from the viewpoint of the organization? What if instead, the organization (as a living thing itself) were to provide the want-list, instead of the typical laundry list of job specs written by HR and/or the hiring manager? What if we actually treated organization's needs with respect and consideration. This would truly be a revolutionary change in the way we view both leadership and organizational dynamics.

It turns out that organizations, small, medium, large, and Fortune-list huge, all have similar fundamental needs. The people who fill those needs best are the ones who feel, deep inside, a connection to the specific organizational need that they are serving. This is what gives a person the sense that they are making a meaningful contribution, moreso than anything else they might be doing. People may do various kinds of work with similar focus and thoughtfulness, but they experience different kinds of work in different ways, each aligned with the specific need of the organization that they, deep down, feel called to fill. This has especially important relevance to leadership.

There are those who are drawn to create big visions, as an entirely new product, or service, or level of awareness. They start an organization as a way to draw other people in to make it happen. In the language of Teamability, they are **Founders**.

There are those who bond to the vision of the Founder and lead the strategic process of putting it on the road to realization. In the language of Teamability, they are **Vision Movers**.

There are those who take the drive and activity of the Vision Mover and shape and form it into a more elegant, efficient framework. This transforms the team as well as the project. In the language of Teamability, they are **Vision Formers**.

There are those who adapt big-picture strategies into action. They are the heroes of their teams as they lead them into the fray. In the language of Teamability, they are **Action Movers**.

And there are those who make sure that every detail is in place, has been accomplished well, and that the project is not closed until everything is done. They are extraordinary project managers, no matter what the project. In the language of Teamability, they are **Action Formers**.

All are leaders. All are essential. If you want to lead, and you feel comfortable in leading, one of these Roles probably resonates with you.

But organizations have five more distinct areas of need, and without them the organization is incomplete and structurally flawed. If you fill one of the other five Roles, you may not be automatically seen as a leader, but that does not mean you can't lead. It may very well be that your organization needs you for a special kind of leading that only you can do.

We're all in this together, and all people were born to serve. Whether your leadership is recognized or not is not so important as your desire to contribute. It is really a matter of finding the right niche.

Here are some tactics you can try along your way to becoming a leader:

- Start, or take a leadership position in, an organization that does something good for people. (I was involved in several parenting nonprofits and learned the good, the bad, the ugly, and the 'well worth the trouble.')

- People often make snap judgments based on how you look, and they're often wrong. But, the more you tune into how they see you, the more you can influence their ideas about you. Ask a friend for feedback. (I will be eternally grateful to my BFF Margot for getting me to stop dressing like a mom, even at business meetings.)

- I have to give credit for this one to serial entrepreneur and investor, Vincent Schiavone. He told me his secret in two words: Get Famous! (I have been working on it ever since. Blogging is a good start!)

- Ask yourself why you want to lead. If your answer is to make more money, there are probably easier ways. If your answer is to change the world, or some part of it, start figuring out how you're going to do that and, more important, who you'll need to team with in order to get there. (Teaming: don't leave home without it.)

- Finally, don't give up. Remember that times change and you will change with them. What is impossible at 30 can be possible at 40, probable at 50, and inevitable at 60. (Just remember as you get older to stay young in your mind, your heart, and your body.)

Leadership is, after all, quite simple. All you have to do is be the person other people <u>want</u> to follow!

@DrJanice: If you want to lead tomorrow, what are you doing today to prepare? #justasking

Afterword

Whatever the occasion, I almost always have at least a few more words. When I thought about what I wanted to share with you, I remembered that I had not yet talked about the inevitable challenges that a leadership journey entails. And that I had not yet cautioned you that no matter what the outcome, you will be transformed by it.

So I will share with you something that I wrote a very long time ago. I thought I was writing it about a mythical 'everyman,' but, of course, as it often happens, I was also warning myself.

This is a story about an amazing journey. There's a roadmap in this story and although it might not be a perfect one for you on your own journey, it can still help you find your way.

The Amazing Journey of the Would-be Hero

Once upon a time there was a Would-be Hero named Workabee. He was a much-appreciated employee at Honeywerx, where he managed a very small unit that made very small products for a very small market.

Workabee loved his job, but he was ambitious. And he loved to listen to the buzz around the Executive Suite, even though he had to wait to get it second-hand from Betty, his Assistant Manager. Sometimes that took a long time, and the buzz had lost some of its buzziness by the time he heard it, since he had to wait until Betty got it from Gloria, her friend in Marketing whose desk was right outside the Executive Suite.

The latest buzz Betty got from Gloria was that the denizens of the Executive Suite were getting long in the stinger and would soon be looking at moving on and making room for their followers. They called this the Opportunity.

Betty was happy to share this delicious morsel with Workabee because he was always so thankful and would think kind thoughts about her, which was exactly how she liked to be thought of.

Workabee had long dreamt of the Opportunity, although he was not exactly sure what it would entail. He knew somewhere deep inside his very being that it was part of his Destiny, although he was not quite sure what that was either.

His stinger was dragging a bit as he exited Honeywerx that day. How was he ever going to find the way to the Opportunity? It seemed like an impossible trip to make when he didn't have a map or walking stick or any other of the bits and pieces he imagined would be very, very useful.

His family greeted him at the door, happy to have him safe at home. Later, after the children had been kissed and tucked in for the night, he shared his ambition with Darla, his dear wife. She believed in him and told him so, but she didn't know anything more than what he told her about the Opportunity.

She was more confident than him that he would reach it. She just knew he was worthy and she told him so several times until they both fell fast asleep.

The next morning, Workabee stopped at the little coffee wagon that always parked in front of Honeywerx. It was earlier than usual and he was the only customer.

Suddenly, out of the corner of his eye, he saw a little old man dressed in a rather rag-tag fashion. Workabee was quite sure he had never seen this funny little fellow in any of the Departments at Honeywerx, although of course he had not actually been in all of them. Honeywerx was quite large and there were a lot of people Workabee had not yet met up with.

Workabee, who was generally as pleasant a gentleman as any, smiled at the little fellow as if he did know him. As he smiled, Workabee got the same very warm feeling he always felt when he greeted the people he knew and cared about.

The little fellow came closer and Workabee could see that he was a proud old man, though apparently a very poor one.

Workabee guessed that the rag-tag little fellow was not a Honeywerx employee at all. In fact, he looked like he hadn't had any extra money in a long, long time.

Workabee, who had a large number of obligations that usually left him with only a few extra pennies for special treats from the little coffee wagon was moved on the spot to turn away from the vendor and instead to press his four wee coins into the hand of the rag-tag little man. Not wishing to embarrass the fellow, Workabee smiled quietly, said "Good day" and started walking toward the Honeywerx entrance.

"Workabee," the little man called out, although being so small and so old, it did not seem that anyone else could have heard his willowy voice. Workabee turned around, not quite sure now if he actually had made this small man's acquaintance, perhaps very long ago and very far away.

"Workabee!" The little man repeated his willowy call, this time with a bit more emphasis. Workabee looked intently into the man's twinkling eyes, which were the color of the Northern Sea where he and Darla had honeymooned many years earlier. His attention was riveted. As he gazed into the man's eyes, which were so oceanic Workabee could see the white-frosted surf in his reflection, he stopped wondering how the little fellow knew his name.

"Workabee, thank you for your four gifts of caring. I would like to give you four gifts too." The little man appeared to be destitute and Workabee was feeling he might have made a mistake and made the rag-tag fellow feel obligated to match his small offering.

As he spoke, right before Workabee's eyes, the rags and tags turned into finery of the finest and the stooped little old man stood taller and taller, glowing with hearty vitality and sporting a sparkling aura of wonder.

"You are about to embark on the very same Hero's Journey as I did when I was a younger man managing a very small unit that made very small products for a very small market, much the same as you do now," he asserted. "And, as was done for me, I am here to give you some special advice and some items that might prove useful at some point."

Workabee was far too awed to ask if that had been at Honeywerx or not, and if the now not-so-little man had actually won the Opportunity. Instead, he turned his attention to where the now not-so-rag-tag man was pointing.

It was a very large map with an irregular coastline and lumps and bumps in the least-expected places. It had a slotted-dotted line that had once been very bright dark blue but appeared to have faded to a lighter shade over time.

Exactly how long that time might have been was not immediately apparent. Workabee wondered how old the man was and even what his name was, but he did not ask, fearing the gifts of knowledge might not be given and the Opportunity would be lost to him and Darla forever.

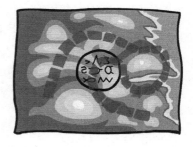

"This is where you start," he said, pointing to a black circle with some mysterious ciphers in its middle, "and this is where you might end." At this last pronouncement of ending, the little man vaguely passed his hand over the whole map.

Allowing his hand to drop to his side, he went on. "In between, if you are lucky, you will meet Four Great Challenges." Workabee had been a dedicated student in the past, but hard as he tried, he was having some trouble interpreting just which of the mysterious lumps or bumps could represent these Four Great Challenges.

"The first of these will definitely be right at the beginning, and you will be able to meet it. In fact you already have, and successfully too, I might add, for I was there when you did it. Perhaps this is a good time to tell you my name, which is First."

Somewhat relieved at knowing his kind benefactor's name, Workabee bowed to First and said, "It is a pleasure to meet you, First. But what, pray tell, is the Great Challenge that I met?"

First smiled his mystifying little smile and answered, "You Moved. You met the Challenge of overcoming the inaction that most people take for granted. It took some courage to come toward me, and a gracious heart to hear what I was saying. But the next Great Challenges you meet may be more difficult for you, so I am going to present you with three gifts in addition to this fine map to guide your Hero's Journey."

Workabee was very proud indeed that he had met a Great Challenge. He could not wait to tell Darla. First could see that Workabee was beginning to seem distracted, so he clapped his hands sharply to bring him back to full attention.

"It looks like you are beginning your Second Great Challenge already, my young friend," First said. A slightly faraway look in his eyes confirmed that he was remembering his own Second Great Challenge and how he used the great gift that had been given him when he was a much younger man.

 Pulling a bit of pink fluff from deep inside his watchpocket, First shook it and teased it into its original form. It had obviously been residing in that watchpocket for a

good many years, although the watch itself had been long gone.

"On the road to the Opportunity you will meet many, many distractions of all sorts," First intoned, "and this will be your protection." Sensing, with certainty, that Workabee had never seen anything like this before and, therefore, would have no idea how useful it could be, First began to explain.

"This is a bit of soft pink cloud to ease the distractions you come upon when you embark on a Hero's Journey. You just put it up over your eyes or ears or wherever you are being distracted and wait until the unwanted desire passes. It's really quite simple to use. The hard part is remembering that you have it and not being so very distracted that you've gone beyond the place where it will still work well."

Workabee remembered times in the past when he had been a tiny bit distracted and had somehow recovered, usually by being reminded by someone or something or someplace. He knew that this would be different, that a Hero must meet much more difficult distractions on his Journey. But he didn't waste time wondering or worrying, since he knew now that First would provide everything he would need and he was anxious to begin.

Once again snapping to attention, Workabee noticed that First was digging way down into one of the lumps or bumps, or maybe it was in one of the valleys, on the map.

Workabee couldn't quite tell what was going on, though it looked as if First was reaching so deep he might get stuck in the in-between place.

Suddenly, with a little popping sound, First emerged whole, with a very small package in his hand.

Watching with great curiosity, Workabee saw First unfold a very intricate-looking packet, carefully smoothing out the plentiful folds and wrinkles. When First was done with his mission, Workabee was looking at a teeny-tiny megaphone. Instead of holding it the way a megaphone is usually held so that a little sound can be made much, much bigger, First had it turned the other way.

"This is always worth the trouble of getting it out of its niche," First said proudly. "Remember, you won't be needing this unless you've successfully passed that Second Great Challenge and don't need that bit of pink cloud any more. This is a little harder to use, but I think you'll enjoy it once you get the hang of it. And nothing works quite as well as when you are meeting that Third Great Challenge. More words and louder words are never a good solution to that one, though that's what most will do. And that's why so few reach that place where their Grandest Opportunity lies waiting for them."

Workabee watched intently so he would be able to remember all the particulars and fine points of operating the megaphone properly. First held it to his mouth, the wide end just covering his lips and the very tippy-tip of his upturned nose.

It seemed to Workabee that First was trying to say something, but in a flash First popped the tiny megaphone in his hand and said, "If all you do remember of this demonstration, dear Journey-Taker, is to hold it the other way than people usually do, you will be ever reminded about the value of silence and keeping your own counsel."

Workabee was silent. Not because he had suddenly encountered his Third Great Challenge before he'd even had a chance to use the bit of pink cloud, but because he was beset with enormity of the Journey before him. But, he reasoned to himself, you will still have First's gifts and counsel to help you. Workabee had an excellent memory and knew it would be reasonably easy for him to summon up First's special voice when he needed him.

Once more, First's activity snapped Workabee to attention. He was skipping along, circling the map, tossing something up in the air and catching it as he gleefully sang a wordless little song of joy. Stopping in front of Workabee, he solemnly pulled a ribbon from his right back pocket and threaded it through a slot at the top of the small object.

Wordlessly, First presented the gift to Workabee. It was a small two-sided disk.

Engraved on one side it read, "I am always with you." On the other side it read, "You are on your own." And at the top was a little swivel contraption that appeared to generate enough energy to cause the little disk to rotate in a seemingly random pattern.

Returning to what Workabee had begun to consider his special voice, First explained the two seemingly contradictory engravings. "It is true," he said, "that I will always be with you," although Workabee had been quite careful not to tell First how he planned to summon up the little fellow's voice whenever he needed him. "But," he continued, "you will also be on your own."

"The Hero's Journey is ultimately a solitary one. There will come a time – we call it the Fourth Great Challenge – when you will have to face an important decision and it will seem to you that I am being silent and not helping you one whit. And you will be quite right about that. It will be then that you meet your Grandest Opportunity at last. It's then that you will look at the engravings and understand how I can be here with you even as you are on your own."

Workabee closed his eyes for just a moment, so overwhelmed was he with the thought of meeting the Four Great Challenges on a successful Hero's Journey. And when he opened his eyes, he found himself at the end of a long line at the coffee wagon in front of the entrance to Honeywerx. That fine little man in his

finery, First, was nowhere to be found. Workabee thought he saw a small old fellow in rag-tag clothing just out of the corner of his eye, but when he turned his head, there was nothing but a swirl of fine dust.

Where the map had been, there was now just a glittering mirage of a deep, sea blue slotted-dotted line. But that didn't matter to Workabee, since with his excellent memory, he could redraw the lumps and bumps and valleys in his head and, besides, he knew where the Opportunity was and how to get there.

The fluffy bit of pink cloud was nowhere to be found, but there was a bit of pinkish string hanging from the middlemost button on Workabee's shirt, so he knew he would remember about not letting the distractions get in his eyes or ears or brain or heart.

Workabee looked around for the tiny little megaphone and could not actually find it, although as he thought about it some more, it felt as if it had become a permanent part of his throat. At the very least, it would serve as a reminder, since it would jingle and jangle to alert him if extra loud words were trying to escape or sneak past.

As the coffee wagon line got shorter and shorter, Workabee remembered why he was there and started thinking about what he needed to do to help his staff with their daily tasks and how he needed to ask Betty, his Assistant Manager, what she thought of the proposed new Very Small Product Line and how they could improve it. But there was one tiny bit of him that was still hoping he could at least find the little disk with the contradictory sayings, one side reading that First would always be with Workabee, and the other that Workabee would also be alone.

The coffee wagon lady looked tired and distracted as Workabee finally reached the little window. Still a bit confused about what had transpired, Workabee was happy to see her familiar face. He did believe that what had happened with First was real, but he was a bit perturbed that the gifts were not quite as he had thought they were.

"One regular coffee and a very small sweetcake," he said, putting his hand into the pocket where he kept the small coins he had brought for this treat. Suddenly, with a shock, he realized that he had given those coins to First and had none in any of his pockets to give to the coffee wagon lady.

He looked around for First, then remembered the words on the side that was turned face up in his heart, where the little disk was now in permanent residence: "You are on your own." He looked up at the coffee wagon lady, intending to apologize for his mistake.

Before the first word could come out of his mouth, she said, "I saw what happened." Workabee's face lit up with joy. His experience was being corroborated, so maybe she would also know what happened to First and his gifts.

Then she continued, her smile growing wider and brighter until she fairly shook with delight. "Please, please take this humble snack from me as thanks for what you did." "What I did?" Now Workabee was even more confused, because he had forgotten about his encounter with the little old rag-tag fellow, before he knew him as First.

"That was my Father who you gave your coins to. He comes around sometimes to see that I am feeling secure and happy, usually when I am feeling neither secure nor happy. He doesn't always look like he is watching over me, but I know he is. And when he leaves, if he has received some small token of respect, like the coins you gave him, something magical always happens. So a cup of coffee and a very small sweetcake are my way of being part of the magic."

Workabee smiled back and headed for the Honeywerx gate. No more words needed to pass between him and the coffee wagon lady.

He felt the disk with the contradictory engravings revolving in his heart as he walked through the gate, following the map of the Hero's Journey to the Opportunity that would be his.

This is Your Journey

The end of this story is really the beginning of the next Great Challenge of your life. You can choose to make this a solitary journey or you can choose to make it in the company of others.

If you choose to make your journey as part of a team, being with people who share the Vision will maximize both your value to others and the value of others to you. And if you choose to make it a solitary journey, the closer the path is to your own mission, the more satisfying and productive one it will be.

Either way, may it bring you to a place of satisfaction and fulfillment.

Acknowledgements

While a book may have one author, it is never really the work of one person. The overt and subtle influences of others are profound, before and during the thinking and writing that becomes the final product. While the people in my life have been many, these get the shout outs for inspiring this book:

Dr. Jack Gerber, Curator, collaborator, and treasured friend, who has worked with me for over 25 years and even at the most difficult times, never lost faith in our vision of making the workplace a better place to work.

Mark Talaba, Vision Former and so much more, who takes my wildest ideas and somehow manages to shape them into something that works elegantly.

Paul Sevcik, Communicator, and Jenny Periquito, Conductor, our first employees. They live the power of teaming on a daily basis, while managing TGI's client and partner services, our internship and coursework programs, our business processes, and everything else that needs doing. (In the midst of all that, they also find enough time to remind me of what's truly important.)

Our investors – Tom Thomson, Bill Puryear, Ray Celli, Tom Talaba, Don Patrick, Rick Zabor, Darryl King, Brittany Blacklidge, Greg Sparzo, and John Altamura – for believing in the vision and supporting its growth.

And, as always, Barry, for telling me I was a born entrepreneur even before I really knew it and loving me through good times and bad.

About the Author

Dr. Janice Presser was raised to be a wife and mother. Both compliant and contrarian, she fulfilled those jobs over the ensuing decades while adding a few more titles to her resume. These have included talent scientist, entrepreneur, family therapist, author of five books on family matters, CEO, technology architect, consultant, blogger, underground midwife, political candidate, and more – and she's not finished yet. Who better to inspire you to go beyond the limits and achieve your wildest dreams?

Dr. Presser can be reached via Twitter by adding @DrJanice to a tweet; at The Gabriel Institute +1.215.825.2500; or by email to DrJanice@thegabrielinstitute.com

Photo: Tom Thomson